To: Sis- Renee
This is your time!
Seize it.

Aaron Yoder

The Advantage of Now

His Purpose in You in Time

RAMON O. GORDON

WESTBOW
PRESS®
A DIVISION OF THOMAS NELSON
& ZONDERVAN

Copyright © 2018 Ramon O. Gordon.

All rights reserved. No part of this book may be used or reproduced by any means, graphic, electronic, or mechanical, including photocopying, recording, taping or by any information storage retrieval system without the written permission of the author except in the case of brief quotations embodied in critical articles and reviews.

This book is a work of non-fiction. Unless otherwise noted, the author and the publisher make no explicit guarantees as to the accuracy of the information contained in this book and in some cases, names of people and places have been altered to protect their privacy.

Scripture taken from the King James Version of the Bible.

Scripture quotations are from the ESV® Bible (The Holy Bible, English Standard Version®), copyright © 2001 by Crossway, a publishing ministry of Good News Publishers. Used by permission. All rights reserved.

Scripture taken from the Amplified Bible, Copyright © 1954, 1958, 1962, 1964, 1965, 1987 by The Lockman Foundation. Used by permission.

Scriptures taken from the Holy Bible, New International Version®, NIV®. Copyright © 1973, 1978, 1984, 2011 by Biblica, Inc.™ Used by permission of Zondervan. All rights reserved worldwide. www.zondervan.com The "NIV" and "New International Version" are trademarks registered in the United States Patent and Trademark Office by Biblica, Inc.

WestBow Press books may be ordered through booksellers or by contacting:

WestBow Press
A Division of Thomas Nelson & Zondervan
1663 Liberty Drive
Bloomington, IN 47403
www.westbowpress.com
1 (866) 928-1240

Because of the dynamic nature of the Internet, any web addresses or links contained in this book may have changed since publication and may no longer be valid. The views expressed in this work are solely those of the author and do not necessarily reflect the views of the publisher, and the publisher hereby disclaims any responsibility for them.

Any people depicted in stock imagery provided by Thinkstock are models, and such images are being used for illustrative purposes only. Certain stock imagery © Thinkstock.

ISBN: 978-1-9736-0888-2 (sc)
ISBN: 978-1-9736-0889-9 (e)

Library of Congress Control Number: 2017918000

Print information available on the last page.

WestBow Press rev. date: 02/16/2018

Contents

Acknowledgments vii
Introduction xi
Chapter 1   Time Uninterrupted 1
Chapter 2   Be Busy at Purpose 14
Chapter 3   You Have the Advantage 31
Chapter 4   Your Move 42
Chapter 5   It Begins with a Dream 55
Chapter 6   Faith Gives You the Advantage 66
Chapter 7   Giant Advantages 78
Chapter 8   What's in Your Hand? 91
Chapter 9   Placement and Promise 104
Chapter 10 Out of a Thought 113
Chapter 11 What about the Rest of You? 123
Chapter 12 The Advantage of Now, Not Next! 134
About the Author 149

Acknowledgments

I would like to dedicate this book to my dear wife, Abigail. Your voice has pierced through much darkness and brought me into a greater sense of consciousness. I love you! Also to my three precious daughters—Emma, Beverly, and Olivia—your unconditional love has only taught me to become a better man. Daddy loves you all! To my church family, Kairos Empowerment Church, I am a better pastor because of you! Thank you for giving me a chance to lead. I love you all!

Praises for The Advantage of Now

"The Advantage of Now gives a spiritual and psychological, yet very logical breakdown of why many remain defeated and are unaware of what season and place God has them in. I believe that in this book lies a key for many who are searching for direction and answers from God can look at their decision making processes and see how they were nonchalant or negligent with their time and in their focus. Pastor Ramon Gordon analyzes what many overlook as a very key variable in moving ahead and being effective in life, which is the "Now" factor! These very wise and prudent words can help add years and meaning to your life by causing you to redeem the time and reset focus back into alignment with the purpose and plan of God."

- Michael A. McClelland,
Senior Pastor All Nations Christian Church,
Newnan Georgia

"Time is one of the greatest resources given from God. Yet, it seems the more we advance in the Information Age, the more scarce our time becomes. This dichotomy provokes many to invest in innovative technologies and training with the hope of harnessing time to no avail. It is high time we consider the possibility that we are approaching the notion of time all wrong. In The Advantage of Now, Pastor Ramon O. Gordon brilliantly redirects the conversation on time, empowering the reader to shift from reliance on information to embodiment of revelation. Chock-full of biblically astute and practical instruction, this must-read inextricably invokes a sense of urgency and peace; and promotes a conscious and intentional awakening and accountability to the purposes and plans of God for our lives. This book is the antidote for the misuse, mismanagement, and misappropriation of time; and the key to transformed, "Kairos living."

Laray E. Dyer, MS, MDiv, PMP
President & CEO, Convergence Worldwide, Inc.

Introduction

Is it time yet? Are we there yet? Those are the questions my daughters asked me as we drove to Orlando for a family vacation. My wife and I decided to take the girls to Disney World for our oldest daughter's birthday. The girls could not contain their excitement, they were so excited that the questions would not stop flowing! Although we were on our way, we had three hours remaining in our car ride until we arrived.

The wait seemed unbearable to the girls at times, but that did not diminish their excitement. The journey that God has you on can be daunting at times. Red lights, alternate routes, traffic jams, and even accidents all play a role in becoming all that God has planned for you. But no matter what, don't lose your excitement.

This book is for people who are ready to do something great with their time on earth. It is about bringing the reader into the consciousness of time and its real purpose. It is easy to live for years with no sense of urgency to act on the vision for our lives, leaving many people unfulfilled and bitter.

This book is written for those who are serious about taking their lives back from fear, indecision, and regret and use whatever time is remaining to use the gifts that God has given them.

In this book, you will see practical and spiritual applications that will offer the reader insight into the timing of God, as well as the human responsibility to act on God's word. With every tick of the clock and passing of the seasons, there must be a consciousness of your purpose and destiny.

This book will teach you how to cultivate the awareness of your gifts, talents, and callings, as you move towards your life's fulfillment.

Many of the principles you will read are taken from sacred scripture. There you will see how we are instructed through the lives of others how to live in the now. You will learn how to be present in the moment, knowing that it is this moment and this moment only that you will ever have in your hands.

Time Uninterrupted

Time is a language; it is like a stream that carries the rich source of water to our vast ocean. It flows uninterrupted and freely.

—Ramon O. Gordon

Red lights met me as I raced to get to a very important meeting down Interstate 85. I was late, horribly behind schedule. And I knew I left at the right time. Well, I thought I did. I had a meeting with a local radio station to talk about getting a time slot for our ministry.

I wanted to explore other facets to expose our ministry to a greater audience. Atlanta traffic can be draining, especially when you are in a rush. So leaving way ahead of time for anything in this city is your best shot at getting there at the right time.

Breathless, the producer met me at the door and said, *"I'm running late. Will be done in thirty minutes."*

Apparently, he had a meeting he forgot about, and I had to wait until he was done so we could speak. Let's recap. I was running late, racing down the freeway to get to this meeting, not knowing he was running late at the studio. If I knew he would be late, I would have changed my pace a little with a sense of peace, knowing I wouldn't have to rush to get there, but we would have our meeting when I arrived. And the producer would have modified his schedule as well so we could meet at the right time.

Time must be communicated, and when not, chaos rules. Time is language; it is like a stream that carries the rich source of water to our vast ocean. It flows uninterrupted and freely. It does not wait for a response, and it does not need validation. Time is that invisible stream that flows through our lives, and if we mishandle its innocence, we will miss opportunities that will afford us the maximized life.

Chaos and regret are the inevitable results of mismanaged time. The ramifications can be painful when the fatal reality of what could have been now exists in our dream container, the place where filtered dreams live, the site where dreamers have the vivid imagination to live in the dream but lack the courage to live out the dream. Ecclesiastes 9: 11 (ESV) says, *"Again I saw that under the sun the race is not to the swift, nor the battle to the strong, nor bread to the wise, nor riches to the intelligent, nor favor to those with knowledge, but time and chance happen to them all."*

According to this scripture, human beings have two things in common. Everyone who has ever lived has met both time and chance. It is not how fast you run, how strong you are, how smart you are, or even how much you know. Everyone has a time to live and a chance to make something happen. Have you ever heard the phrase, "Take a chance"? It means to risk something. Every person is given this precious commodity called time, and it is up to him or her to use it wisely. We cannot stop time, but humans can control its use by using their gifts and talents to make an impact on the earth.

Out of seven billion people on this planet, you have a distinct purpose set by God to use your time wisely. Not everyone lives the same amount of years or has the same gifts. But each person has the opportunity of time. It is critical to understand that God dwells in eternity and is not controlled by time. He is outside of time, and time is His servant. Isaiah 57:15 (KJV) says, *"For thus saith the high and lofty One that inhabiteth eternity, whose name is holy."* Not only does God dwell in the high and holy place but the second clause of Isaiah 57:15

says, God, dwells with him that is of a contrite and humble spirit. God is omnipresent. He is everywhere at the same. He is not limited to time and space but fills and controls both time and space.

God does not function according to the minute and hour hand on the clock, but He is outside of the constraints and restraints of time. Therefore, when God speaks, He expresses from a completed place. Nothing needs to be improved from Gods perspective. Genesis 1:31 KJV, *"And God saw everything that he had made and, behold, it was very good."* God manifests in time what has already been completed in eternity. This is truly the primary function of time, to see the manifestation of the will of God for your life. Be encouraged today, my fellow believer, that all the plans of God for your life originated in a place not controlled by time. Shake off anxiety, and put your faith in God.

From Chronos to Kairos

The Greeks used two words for time: Chronos and Kairos. Chronos is measurable time, quantitative, or clock time. Kairos is the opportune time or the right time. German theologian, Paul Tillich referred to Kairos as a historical moment in his book A History of Christian Thought. It is a moment of qualitative meaning, the quality of the moment that demands that the world pays attention. The Kairos moment is that moment when God infuses an individual with incredible courage to break through the ordinary rules of life and seize the moment. In effect, that Kairos moment is like a "aha moment", the moment when you wake up your truths. These are the truths that only you can take accountability for; it is a place of awareness that surrounds your everyday life.

Chronos can be defined as the timing of the natural order. It refers to minutes and seconds, measurable time, or time that repeats itself. A friend may tell you that she will pick you up at six thirty. This time is measured according to her plans and arrangements; however, that time can easily change because of unforeseen events leading up to that time. You can never have a grasp on time because it was not designed for that. Time is not some tangible thing that you can see, touch, or smell. The best way to define time is that it is easily gone when you are not conscious of its existence. I believe that God has given every man and woman a Kairos moment, a moment where history is made. It is up to you to discern the time and move in this time with an unapologetic faith.

Timing requires consciousness so actions can be executed with undistorted motives and a true sense of purpose. The past is fixed, and the future awaits you, but now is the moment that you must maximize to fulfill the purpose for which you are created. We operate in Chronos (clock time), but we function with a Kairos mentality. You have to operate knowing it is not length of days or years, but at any moment, something wonderful could happen. This is the truth of now, knowing that this moment is the most precious instant that your creator has given you.

No matter who is reading this or wherever it is being read, you have the power to do something with your now. Someone may read this book five to ten years from now, and it will still have the same impact that it had five to ten years earlier. To understand the power of now, you must first understand the power of the mind and the responsibility that the mind has to engage the opportunities that the time presents.

Winning the battle requires we use our hands and feet to achieve that victory. I have heard many people say they won the battle in the mind, but their reality is a staunch opponent of what they profess with their mouths. Like converting improper fractions into whole numbers, words must be converted into action.

Now is your advantage. The present place and state of your existence is the place where conscious decisions must be made. Whether you are in a broken marriage or in financial lows, you have to make decisions today that will strengthen your results tomorrow. The agony of making the pronouncement is more tolerable than enduring the consequences of indecision. I hate consequences, especially those produced by my behavior. Here is the first step toward progress, decisions. It is making the decision even when that choice is hard.

Our mindset has to change to accommodate what God is going to do in our lives. If we do not shift our mindset, we miss another opportunity and another year to do what God told us to do. Chronos thinking, the thinking that the Greeks regarded as qualitative time, is laced within the fabric of the natural order. It does not respond to faith; it reacts to reason.

Oftentimes we plan to do things in our Chronos experience without considering the mind of God for our lives. We make geographical moves, buy houses, make business investments, and even get married. However, it is not our plans that determine destiny; rather it is God's plan for our lives that determine our destiny. The key here is to put God as first in your life. Make Him a priority before anything or anyone in your life.

A Right Attitude

The right attitude can get you through your day and the various challenges that the day presents. Herein lies the secret to allowing the peace of God to rule your life. A Kairos mentality is simply an attitude that embraces the best to come even when that moment has yet to arrive. It is an attitude that keeps you fixed on developing your gift and talents while you are waiting, even if it seems like others have surpassed you in their endeavors. It is a state of mind that is worth developing because of the benefits it brings, including peace, optimism, expectation, and joy.

The right attitude can clear your mental space so you can be in the proper state of mind to see and seize those opportune moments. You begin to expect success and not failure. You see solutions for the problems you face, and you start to fix your focus on better things to come. Having the right attitude is not merely saying it, but acting it out in your everyday life challenges. Developing the right outlook is one of the most powerful assets we can have. We all want success, good health, wealth, and a prosperous future for our children, and healthy marriages, and these can be obtained with the right attitude.

• Once you channel your energy toward positive things, you will see positive things happen. The law of attraction simply says you attract what you think. Positive thoughts will produce positive results, while negative thoughts will produce negative results. With the right attitude, the right sensitivity can be developed for discerning the right opportunities.•

To seize every moment that God has for us, we must shift from faith to works. In other words, we must go from thought to action. That action decides that Kairos moment. Yes, it is true that, without faith, it is impossible to please God, but faith will only remain a hope if the will is not engaged. For faith to reach its expectation, which is manifestation, it must get aggressive in the Chronos with a Kairos mentality.

Please understand that everyone has an appointed time, a moment set aside for you to do your thing with your zest and charisma with God's anointing all over you. Faith is potential, and works is the exercise of that potential. God gives everyone the ability to believe according to what He has placed in him or her. •

Often God will interrupt the flow of normalcy in our lives so he can reveal a greater way to us. For God's Word to be revelatory, it has to be God-infused. In other words, God will unveil the secrets in His Word so, when it collides with the hearts of men, it becomes revelation. Once we adapt ourselves to an attitude of normalcy, we become callous and insensitive to the leading of God.

Respect Time

Time is one of the most valuable resources that God has given to man. It is a precious gift. We must respect time if we are going to be truly effective at living the existence that God has designed us to live. When time is respected, it will be managed effectively, since we are all managers of the time God has given us to live out. Always remember that God is the author and finisher of all things that pertain to our lives. The scripture says, *"The steps of a good man are ordered by the Lord"* (Psalm 37:23 KJV). This scripture implies that God has arranged every step of our lives with purposeful intent. God orders all our victories, tears, and mistakes. Nothing surprised Him or caught Him off guard.

When we respect time, we approach its innocence gingerly and purposely. This attitude works for the believer as he or she embraces the plans that God has for their life. We can easily exist and not live. Sadly, this is not God's will. He does not want us to take up space; He wants us to use our space as a platform to live our lives to the best of our abilities and with the tools we have been given.

Do you value your time? You must explore this question in your personal lives. I have found out that I have disrespected my time on many occasions. I possessed this slacking-off mentality that stalled my progress on many levels.

To avoid this slacking-off syndrome, you must redefine why you are doing what you are doing, and you must respect the thing you do with the time you have. For example, spending time with your family is vital for a healthy family life. However, if you do not respect time, setting aside a time for family will be of least importance. What you give respect to decides how you manage your time.

Not all use of time is equal. So, the thing you spend the time with the most will produce the most effective results. If you spend more time doing what is profitable, then you build on your passions and goals for your life. If you spend your time watching television, browsing the internet, then you have become effective at doing nothing. You see, either way, you are effective. Whether you want more wealth, more thrill in life, or more success, it is all based on how you spend your time.

Manage Your Time

Once you understand the importance of respecting time, you can now set the guidelines to manage your time. As I noted before, mismanagement of time will yield no results and can produce a bitter end. To avoid becoming the latter, you must make the best of our time now.* Part of our unique human nature is that we are instinctive by that very same nature. We respond to impulses and whatever is being transmitted to our psyche. This means you must choose to entertain options that point towards your destiny.

It would be easier if all of life's choices were filtered as great choices, but life does not offer that luxury. You will be presented with the good and the bad, the clear and the distorted, yet you must decide. Time management is most appreciated when you have chosen wrong before, now, you have the experience and can make wiser choices the next time around. Lounging over a decision that does not fit the vision for your life will only frustrate and prolong the move of God in your life. No one can predict life. It throws us curveballs from time to time. However, a lack of prediction does not excuse a plan of action for your life.

With a plan comes accountability, and you will live effectively and consciously when you know that this is your time to do something that will bring glory to God on the earth. When you are a manager of your time, you will set a system in place to help foster the necessary environment for your goals.

Your vision came from God; therefore, you will need the sense of divinity in your environment, so you can thrive in the peace that is released while you work on your project. Surrounding yourself with a healthy church community can be good grounds for you to thrive as well. The combination of spirituality and productivity with your planning will create an atmosphere where your ideas can thrive in the infancy of its development. There is no such thing in finding time because time cannot run out. That should never be your approach to time, rather, it should be, active engagement in your life's vision at the very moment you believe it's your time.

The problem that so many people run into is that they do not condense their vision into a stratagem of ideas and goals. It will become easier to manage our time when we do not overload ourselves with unrealistic expectations. Take it one step at a time. Once you manage your time correctly, you will see the right people, opportunities, and resources make their way into your life.

Convert Yourself

Because time is constant, needing no modification, time functions at its highest level of perfection. Time does not need converting, but what is needed is an understanding of personal conversion. The root meaning of the word convert is change. Whether someone is changing religious beliefs or changing dollars to euros, it's the same concept. It becomes important to implement personal conversions in your life- these are intimate moments that can redefine you completely.

Missed opportunities do not mean you are out of time, but it does suggest that there must be an urgency to capitalize on your next move. Between the missed opportunity and your next move should be the conscious conversion of yourself. This action is a constructive self-appraisal that will reveal the brilliance of who God made you to be.

We will not always use time to the best of our abilities, but once you know your purpose and you are driven by that awareness, you will consciously decide to use all your cognitive energy to do what must be done. Never let failure determine how far you go, but use that experience as a rotor that propels you forward.

The mistake that many people make is they quit the pursuit of their dreams because of a blunder. While I do believe that integrity is a vital attribute, people are not disqualified because of serious character flaws. *"For though the righteous fall seven times, they rise again."* (Proverbs 24:16 NIV). The man that this scripture speaks about could be anyone of us, but the scripture also gives us a direction, and that is upward.

Rising is the only choice after a fall, so learn to convert:

- your negative experiences into a positive testimony that can strengthen somebody else;
- your mistakes into lessons learned for the next opportunity that is heading to you right now; and
- your downtime into productive initiatives.

On those days filled with boredom and a lethargic approach to life, muster up the passion as you build on the vision for your life. Not doing anything today sets the tone for how you approach your vision tomorrow. Discipline plays a role in how you think and ultimately carry out that thought. So, think purposely, and plan to execute the proper plans in place for your success.

Kairos: A Lifestyle

You cannot truly live with a sense of Kairos with a passive approach to getting things done. Passivity will not work here; nor will some mystical energy. It is not the waving of the hand or the Christian workouts that we see in our churches. Even the Great Commission gives the disciples a directive in Matthew 28:19-20 (KJV), *"Therefore go and make disciples of all nations, baptizing them in the name of the Father and of the Son and of the Holy Spirit, and teaching them to obey everything I have commanded you. And surely, I am with you always, to the very end of the age."*

The world is not coming to you, but you must go and affect your world. It is the responsibility of every child of God to go out and engage the world with the love of God. Like many, I enjoy the worship experience in our churches, but there must be a translation from the worship experience in the church building to the everyday reality of life outside of that religious construct. The difficulty for many churchgoers today is taking the intimacy in our worship experience into our busy day-to-day lives.

Praise without practicing spiritual principles will only result in ignorant living. Unfortunately, we begin to adapt the attitude that God will do, and we miss the spiritual truth that God has already completed His will for our lives before the worlds were even framed. There must be an urgency to act on what God has already done. It is what Dr. King called *"the fierce urgency of now."* Go into all the world. There is no limit to where He is sending you. God ignites you with fresh zeal, empowers you with His Spirit, and sends you out to engage. Ignite, Empower, Engage.

The Advantage of Now

Purposeful living is when you are conscious of the times and you use your gifts to answer the voids in your generation. Conscious Kairos living will require deliberate action now. Stop waiting to respond to the right moment, and react to what has been lying dormant in your spirit. Jesus said, *"I must work the works of him that sent me, while it is day: the night cometh, when no man can work"* (John 9:4 KJV).

When Jesus speaks about night in the text, He is speaking about His inevitable trial and crucifixion. Each miracle He performed will attract notoriety as well as condemnation, ultimately hastening the divine culmination of His assignment on earth. Jesus understood that He had a window to function for God before His crucifixion. So, He had to work the works! What a mindset! Jesus worked for the Father and was solely focused on completing the Father's will. He was not bothered by the opinions and expectations or even the traditions of others, but remained unmoved by the distractions. Jesus knew why He was on the earth at that time, and it was that awareness that guided Him.

Remember when Jesus rebuked Peter? See Mark 8:33. Peter heard Jesus speak about His inevitable death, and the words Jesus spoke displeased Peter deeply, so much so that Peter began to rebuke the Messiah. Peter was trying to talk Jesus out of His mission, but this was why He came to the earth. There will be times when people will try to speak you out of your destiny. But you must be resolute like Jesus was, and decide you will not let others' concerns become a stumbling block to your progress. However genuine those concerns may be, there are just some destiny paths that love cannot dismiss.

Peter responded out of emotion, and he was not sensitive to the Spirit of God. We will have some Peters in our lives, who love us and mean us well, but they will be insensitive to God's will for our lives from time to time. Peter, the one who loved Jesus so much, ended up being a major pillar in the church until this day and the ages to come. You may have a Peter in your circle who may not understand why you must bear your cross, but that is never grounds for you to hinder your metamorphosis into destiny. Stay on the path.

Ramon O. Gordon

For This Time: Remember Esther

Unexpected things happen for people who were never considered in the first place. Here is what is so wonderful about God. He chooses who and when He pleases, and He uses them how He pleases. Remember Esther? A Jewish orphan wins the heart of the king, only to step into the kingdom at a strategic time to be a voice for the Jewish people. There was a reason why Queen Vashti did not dance for the king, which ultimately led the king to divorce her. (See Esther 1.)

Every step about your life was not happenstance, but rather a step of purpose towards your destiny.

Timing is a powerful theme in the book of Esther. As you read this wonderfully crafted story, you will see how time unfolds, and the destiny of this young girl is revealed. *"If you keep quiet at a time like this, deliverance and relief for the Jews will arise from some other place, but you and your relatives will die. Who knows if perhaps you were made queen for just such a time as this?"* (Esther 4:14 NLT).

Esther would become queen at a pivotal time when the Jewish people were under much hostility. Haman, the king's second-in-command, wanted the Jews destroyed, and he manipulated the king to call for execution. But God had a Jewish girl in place who would change the heart of a king and alter the course of history for a nation.

Could it be that, at this very moment, God is creating a Vashti scenario in your life? Someone else's rejection is paving the way for your acceptance. God has already spoken to your boss about your increase, and things are happening behind the scenes that you know nothing about. God manipulates time and circumstances to fit you in a position to reign. If Esther had the slightest idea that she would be queen, she would wake up every morning, looking in the direction of the palace.

But sometimes God keeps the palace a secret to you until it is the right time. Like Esther, many of you have a destiny to be a voice for a generation. Now is your time to conquer fear and mount the saddles of faith. Could it be your time? Yes, it is. Your destiny is so much bigger that you and each step you take is tailor made just for you.

The Advantage of Now

As you read this, things are unfolding for you right now. God has set you in place on purpose, and he will need your voice to echo justice and faith to anyone and everyone who will hear you. The providence of God fit Esther in place for favor and influence. Nothing could deter Esther from her path. Have you come to the kingdom for such a time as this? Even during opposition, God has called you to a high place. Like Esther, you are in place at the right time with God's favor backing you.

Now is the time to be empowered! Not yesterday, but today. Yesterday only serves as a reference for future successes. God has given us the future to live the fulfilled life. My prayer is that, as you read this book, you will take advantage of the time God has given you.

Be Busy at Purpose

Choose to be busy with activities that endorse destiny fulfillment, or your life will just speak noise.
—Ramon O. Gordon

This chapter is for those whose lives seem busy, but being busy can simply be noise without production. This too many times has been the tragedy of a busy life when we are busy at doing everything else but the purpose for which we have been created. The real issue is not time but rather our attitudes towards time.

Many of us have fallen victim to being busy and have lived conveniently and not purposefully. Oftentimes we have this unhealthy compulsion to save time, but time does not work that way. Staying busy at just anything does not safeguard personal fulfillment. You must bring your consciousness into play and start working from that place of awareness.

There is no shortage in time. The issue with many is how time is perceived. When an individual does not manage his or her time well, it means that he or she is a poor manager of time, which I also label as time-poor individuals. Time-poor is the category of people who blame their ineffectiveness on a lack of time itself. It could mean that your list of things to do can keep you so busy that you produce nothing meaningful at the end of the day.

The Advantage of Now

Typically, this is what you hear from time-poor individuals, "I don't have time to do ..." Having a full schedule does not mean strategic planning for success. It just means our current culture has taught us always to be engaged in doing something. Look busy. However, looking busy does not mean you are fulfilling destiny.

We live in a society where our worth seems to be placed on how much we have; how many times our phones chime; how many likes we got on our Facebook post; or how many followers we have on Twitter. The truth is, none of those things matter. The more we simplify our lives, the more time we have to spend on those things that matter, like taking your daughter to her dance recital or going to that PTA meeting.

Highly successful people master the art of simplification, the art of living in the control zone. If you notice the lifestyles of highly successful individuals, you will observe a code that rules their day. Facebook founder, Mark Zuckerberg, has a daily wardrobe that includes a gray shirt and jeans. Steve Jobs wore a turtleneck and jeans almost daily. They understood what was important and they spent their time executing their vision. Wearing Gucci or Prada shoes are just the extra trimmings of success, but the real success lies in what motivates someone to get up every morning with the mindset to work their vision.

> *Give me six hours to chop down a tree and I will spend the first four sharpening the axe.*
> —Abraham Lincoln

Spend less time in your execution and more time in planning your life. Conserve your energy. Make sure that you give your attention to what can propel you. Know your worth and know it's worth- the energy you invest into something meaningless will only frustrate you in the long term. Muhammad Ali, arguably the greatest boxer to have ever lived knew about conserving energy. He used strategy in the boxing ring. "Rumble in the Jungle" was arguably one of the greatest sports spectacle of the twenty-first century. Muhammad Ali knocked out George Foreman on October 30, 1974, in Kinshasa, Zaire.

Ali called his strategy the rope-a-dope, where he would lean into the ropes and cover up, allowing Foreman to unleash a barrage of body blows; however, this strategy would weaken Foreman immensely. On the ropes, it looked like Foreman overpowered Ali, but inside that space, Ali had the advantage, and he would find openings to throw fast jabs to Foreman's face. Always remember that it is never about the opinions of the onlookers yelling, "Get off the ropes." If you stick to your strategy, you will secure your victory. Sometimes you have to be willing to take some blows when you are on your way to victory. It may hurt, and you may stagger, but execute your strategy.

So many people I have met complain about not having enough time or say their job takes up most of the day. These same people claim they know what they have to do but never move on that knowledge. Staying purposefully busy should not produce a strain because of your efforts; rather it should produce a pleasure from seeing your efforts produce positive results.

I believe that God wants us to be busy, and He has set a plan in the scriptures to help bring us into purpose fulfillment. Often those questions that put us on a quest for understanding inundate us. In some sense, it can be an existential crisis that is triggered at conscious stages in a person's life. Questions like: Why am I here? Who am I? What am I meant to do? These inquiries help to bring us into consciousness about who we are and why we are on the earth. Everyone does not always come into the enlightenment of his or her purpose, but once he or she does, choices must be made.

The purpose you feel within is that innate, nagging, conviction that just won't go away. No matter how much you try to deviate from the conviction you feel, purpose yet remains within you. Until you answer that call, you will not find peace and tranquility in your life. This sort of feeling does not go away but stays with you until you respond to it.

The key to staying busy at purpose is knowing where your priorities

The Advantage of Now

lie in life. Arrange your purpose by putting those things that are important in perspective. Family, finances, education, and career are all things that help to develop the right attitude towards establishing the steps to purpose. Each day that passes, there are new opportunities that are available to aid in the choices we make toward purpose fulfillment. Will you say no today, or will it be a yes? Once you know your purpose, you will then spring into action, but every potential action is a potential seed that can either produce good or bad fruit. Not only should you think before you act, but also pray before you act.

From God to Man

The Gospel writer Luke writes from a perspective of Jesus that commands attention. Luke, the physician, captures Jesus's early years, otherwise known as the silent years. During those years, Jesus grows and matures. As a Bible student, I often wonder about Jesus's early years—what He was like and what He did. Luke's account of Jesus' early years helps to carve out a place for my imagination. The Gospel of Luke focuses on Jesus's gradual growth of maturity in Nazareth. The other Gospels present Jesus's life from different perspectives, but we can see the boy Jesus in the gospel of Luke.

Luke gives us a side of Jesus that captures His full humanity, one that is relevant to our human experience. Luke 2:40 (KJV) says, *"And the child grew, and waxed strong in spirit, filled with wisdom: and the grace of God was upon him."*

The first few words of the above-stated Scripture are captivating, *"and the child grew!"* The angel Gabriel said to Mary, *"Hail, thou that art highly favored, the Lord is with thee: blessed art thou among women."* See Luke 1:28 (KJV). This child was the answer to a lost world, one steeped in sin and degradation.

But for this child to be fully prepared for His assignment, He had to grow. Two verbs describe growth: grew and wax strong. The word "grew" is the Greek verb auxano, "to become greater, grow, increase, or become strong." "Wax strong" is the Greek verb krataioo, "become strong." It can refer to physical strength, as it probably does here, as well as psychological and spiritual strength.

Although Jesus was God in the flesh, He was limited in knowledge as a human being but had all knowledge as God. The scripture declares *"but emptied himself, taking on the form of a bond-servant, and being made in the likeness of men"* See Philippians 2:7 (NASB). God was so gracious to give us His Son so we could relate to His life through His humanity. (See Hebrews 4:15.) His humanity became—and still is—the place of relevance for generations prior and those to come. His humanity is where God meets the sinner, justice meets injustice, grace meets law, and love meets hate. Packaged in Jesus was God. Not a fraction, but all of God. Jesus brings God to a world that so desperately needed Him at the time and so desperately needs Him now. (See 2 Corinthians 5:19.)

In truth, before any of us can tackle great feats and pull down great mountains, we first must grow and develop in our character. Before we can see the fulfillment of God's plan for our lives, we must grow through growing seasons. *"And the child grew."* Luke was not just speaking about Jesus's natural growth, but he was also talking about His spiritual growth. The two were both working simultaneously at the same time. Natural and spiritual were both developing.

In one world, His limbs were developing, His hair was growing, and His features were changing. And in another world, the world of the Spirit, His insight, and attentiveness to the things of God were growing. Now in the scriptures, Jesus was probably around the age of twelve, which then would place Him at the start of puberty. Yes, the God-man, the one who existed before Abraham, the one who was before the beginning, grew.

Jesus grew, and God's grace was upon Him. I would like to note, before Jesus came to the earth, His purpose was already in His assignment. The meaning for why He came was not lodged in some distant place, but it was inherent in Him. It was in His name.

Matthew 1:21 (KJV) says, *"And she shall bring forth a son, and thou shall call his name Jesus: for he shall save his people from their sins."*

The Advantage of Now

The name of Jesus means salvation, or it is translated in the Greek language as "Jehovah is salvation." It means that Jesus is the source of God's deliverance. Jesus's purpose and destiny were already written in eternity before He got here. I want you to know that, just like Jesus, you have purpose wired into you at this very moment. It is not trying to get in you. God the Father has already implanted it into you.

The moment you got here, your season began. However, knowing your purpose does not always guarantee that you will fulfill that purpose in your season. It is going to take an active awareness and preparation to fully engage the season that God is unfolding in your life. As God is raising you up to bring change to the world, embrace the changes that come with the seasons of your life. An honest appraisal of the changes in your life will bring into focus the personal evolution you must make to accommodate the change.

Whenever Jesus' name is mentioned, we know why He came and what His mission was. A name just does not identify a person, but it pinpoints their calling and ultimately their reason for living. What legacy do you want your name to leave? Will it be a history of inaction or a legacy of lasting change that affects another generation? Let us choose the latter and determine to live our lives as Christ lived.

Where Is Jesus?

Jesus was twelve years old when He disappeared in Jerusalem at the feast of the Passover. According to the scriptures, this was not the first time that his parents made this pilgrimage. They did this many times before, this time was different, however. His parents would see that the boy Jesus had a purpose that was on the brink of fulfillment, and their feelings toward it did not matter.

Jesus stays in Jerusalem while Mary and Joseph make the journey back to Nazareth. A whole day's journey went by before they noticed that Jesus was not there. Here is a quick note for purpose-minded people. When you do not focus on His person, you lose His presence.

And every purpose-minded individual needs His presence. It is a necessary component to our growth and development.

You have to know where you do not fit if you are going to live a life of distinction. When you understand this, living purpose-minded becomes easier and more acceptable to you. People who are not purpose-conscious become trapped in the flow of ordinary living, and they are caught in the panic and confusion of losing something valuable. Luke 2:44 (KJV) says, *"But they, supposing him to have been in the company, went a day's journey; and they sought him among their kinsfolk and acquaintance."* The purpose of God will take you out of what is familiar into what is unfamiliar; unfamiliarity is the breeding ground for true authenticity.

Mary and Joseph looked for Jesus among what was familiar to them, but what was familiar to them was not familiar to Him. From time to time, you will be sought for among your kinsfolk and acquaintances, but you cannot be found because the internal compass of purpose is taking you in another direction. Just because you may be one in blood does not mean you will be one in spirit. The crew you used to hang with in your old neighborhood and play ball with can become unfamiliar to you when that internal compass begins to direct you towards your calling. Oftentimes you will be sought for in places where everybody looks. But you cannot afford to get lost in the familiar when your destiny is calling you out of and into something new.

One would immediately say, "They lost Jesus." But did they? Could it be that Jesus followed His instinct to explore unfamiliar territory and discover new meaning? What is in you that is pulling you away from your familiar and taking you into unfamiliar territory? Your sense of purpose will birth new consciousness within you causing you to explore new environments. It is here that you begin to discover new gifts, talents, and abilities.

❧ In truth, much of who we are cannot manifest because of unbelief. ☙ Jesus could not share His greatness with ordinary-thinking people in His hometown of Nazareth because they had a fixed opinion about

Him. Matthew 13:58 (KJV) says, *"And he did not many mighty works there because of their unbelief."*

Please understand, when people choose not to believe in who you are and what you are doing, it is not your fault. People will choose to believe in who you were and not believe in who you have become. What you are becoming now does not fit their appraisal of what they always knew you to be. Well, that is a clear sign that those individuals no longer belong in your circle. Jesus' parents looked for Him where He was, only to find that He moved to another place. So instead of wasting your energy on getting people to believe you, move on to the next place. Just because you do not see new things manifesting for you in your "Nazareth" does not mean that new things will not manifest for you in your "Jerusalem." Perhaps purpose will navigate you through the different phases and places of your life into what God has ordained for you.

Nazareth was normal for Jesus for a season, but once He started to exhibit the works of God, the clock started ticking on His departure. Whatever is different about you is a threat to somebody else's normal. Believe it or not, this is a part of you becoming busy at purpose. Now you will take your uniqueness into unfamiliar territory where you will find more of a demand placed on your gift. Proverbs 18:16 NKJV says, *"A man's gift makes room for him, and brings him before great men."* However, it is important to note that you cannot walk in the arena of greatness before your gift meets the heavy shackles of rejection. Rejection is simply God's way of taking you from ordinary to greatness. Never look at rejection as the ultimate answer from man because, where man ends, God begins.

The Father's Business

I do not know what prompted Jesus to stay behind while His parents went ahead, but I do believe that Jesus was following the signal of the Holy Spirit, and it landed Him in unfamiliar territory. I will go as far to say that, once you follow the signals of the Holy Spirit, you will always be ahead. In other words, you will always have the advantage. Jesus was busy doing the divine and not the natural. He understood His assignment and had a keen sense of His existence. These two core components drove Him early in His life.

Jesus did not let His earthly association sever His divine connection. I believe this is a message to someone. Do not let your associations on the earth sever your divine connection to God the Father. Jesus said, *"Who is my mother, sister, and brother, those that do the will of God."* See Matthew 12:50 (KJV). To truly be about the Father's business means you have to intentionally become less interested in others' affair.

Doing the Father's business is the perfect remedy to overcoming people. You know, the people factor has been a persistent obstacle for many people. You will have no time to worry about what others are doing when you are destiny minded. Jesus said, *"Did you not see and know that it is necessary [as a duty] for Me to be in My Father's house and [occupied] about My Father's business?"* (Luke 2:49 AMPC).

The prevailing question is: are you about your Father's business? Or have you decided to stay with the predictability of your daily routine? What the Father has called you to should be your focus in life. Although Joseph had a level of authority in Jesus's life, Father God would direct Jesus from within. Some would say Jesus was disrespectful. He needs to be disciplined! Au contraire! Jesus understood something that many of us never grasp, that is, age never dictates spiritual maturity.

Just because you go to church with people who have been there for twenty to thirty years does not mean that they have gotten a revelation about Jesus. Often the people we think are close are far, and the people we think are far are close to the Lord. So, age is never a factor as it relates to our walk with God, it is sensitivity to His role in our lives.

From the tender age of twelve, Jesus followed the divine instinct to tread new ground. The next time your inner circle of family and

The Advantage of Now

friends find you, what will you say to them? Do not apologize for following your instincts into new exposure. Rather, let your boldness be a confirmation that God is working within you.

Vision-Minded

The late Dr. Myles Munroe said. *"Sight is a function of the eyes, but vision is a function of the heart. When a person doesn't have a vision, they live by their eyes. That means we live by what we see. That's one of the reasons why people are so depressed, and that's why the future never becomes a reality."*

Becoming a vision-minded individual is the key to achieving a healthy, purposeful lifestyle. Having a vision becomes the catalyst for intentional, purposeful living. Vision is what God puts on the canvas of your imagination. It is the blueprint for your lives. By vision, we either live or die. Proverbs 29:18 (NIV) says, *"Where there is no vision, the people perish."* Another interpretation of that scripture is, *"Where there is no revelation, people cast off restraint."* Where there is no revelation of the future, people live aimlessly and without focus.

In other words, without vision, life can be chaotic and undeveloped. Your vision is why you behave the way you do. It motivates you to do. Vision is the stimulus that drives you to pursue your goals, and without it, you can live carelessly and aimlessly. A man or woman without a vision tends to live a loose life. Anything goes in that person's life. But a man or woman with vision lives with a sense of frugality. They do not have time for anything that does not endorse their vision for their lives. Vision does three things: disciplines your life, controls your life, and safeguards your focus. People become ungovernable when there is no vision to guide them. If this happens on such a large scale, it is equally as true on a personal level. Every individual needs a vision for his or her life. Your vision,

- Disciplines your life. Discipline can be defined as self-imposed standards for the sake of a higher goal. Another definition of discipline is power under control. It is the ability to bring your senses into submission to God's will for your life. Discipline is training. It is self-control. When you are goals-oriented, self-discipline will develop the ability within you to delay personal gratification. You won't stay up all night partying when you know you have final exams in the morning. You won't have time to criticize the efforts of others, but you will be engaged in your vision. Discipline is not a delay towards personal fulfillment, rather, discipline teaches you to sacrifice with a view to that ultimate reality.

- Vision controls your life. When your vision has arrested you, you now operate with a clear focus. It is easy to let other things control us- unless we take control of our lives through vision. Life is like a current that will bring unexpected challenges downstream. Therefore, you need vision, to bring you into a stable place. Your vision now gives your life a new sense of meaning. No longer are you discouraged by the negative influx of circumstances, because your vision is guiding your life.
- Vision safeguards your future. Your vision should be a clear mental picture of your future. What have you been seeing? It is your responsibility to take accountability for what you see, not anyone else's. Your future self depends on your present self to get it together now. When God reveals something to you, He does this knowing that you will achieve. God knows what he placed in you, but do you? You don't have forever to fulfill our purpose on the earth. Isaiah 46:10 (KJV) says, *"I have made known the end from the beginning."* The path God has set for you has already been established and set in eternity, but you were born to begin the end. The end of your life is waiting for you to begin. The end can only become a goal to be achieved when you step out on your vision. Your vision is the end of yourself meeting the consciousness of the present moment. Take what God is making known to you today and begin.

The Advantage of Now

The attention you give to your vision is the fuel that drives it, and when it is ignored, it cannot produce. Understand that your vision comes from God, the author, and finisher of your faith and ultimately your earthly experience. So, the first thing every visionary must do is pay attention to the one who gave the vision, and he will direct your steps as you walk out what He has placed in your heart. Have a relationship with the one who gave the vision because you will need His power to execute what He has given you.

One of my most favorite scriptures in the Bible says, *"There are many devices in a man's heart; nevertheless, the counsel of the Lord, that shall stand"* (Proverbs 19:21 KJV). The key to understanding this scripture is that all the planning we do does not diminish God's plans for our lives. There is nothing you can do to stop the season God has for you from unfolding, His plan will prevail, because it is His good pleasure.

Exposure

What if Jesus did not get the exposure He got in Jerusalem? What if He went back to Nazareth with His parents and everyone else? Jesus was able to seize the moment and expose Himself to an environment outside of His normal. Possibly if He had procrastinated, He could have missed an opportunity to experience something new.

Be willing to expose yourself to the challenge of the unfamiliar and a novel way of thinking, or you can maintain the current mindset of "happy where I am." The challenge that comes with exposure is that you enter a new arena of worldviews and cultures that force you to expand your thinking. Here, you learn that the system of thought that was your compass for years has now been exposed to unfamiliar territory. Once you find yourself in unfamiliar territory, you must choose to adapt, or you can stay locked in the confinement of your mentality.

All GPS systems are not the same; many are not updated past a certain date. When my wife and I first moved into our first home, it was very difficult to find on the GPS because it was a new subdivision. The GPS took us to a certain point and declared that we arrived at our destination. The only problem was that it was the wrong house. The beautiful thing about the Holy Spirit is that He always knows the will of God for your life. Therefore, if you are sensitive to His guidance, you will go directly to the place on God's spiritual map.

Some people get exposed to what may be unfamiliar to them because of misfortune; others get exposed because of choice. When slaves were brought to America from Africa, their new environment was extremely hostile, and they had to learn to adapt to survive. Adaptation is necessary for survival in any situation, and this has been true from the beginning of time. Even Jesus had to adapt during His life on earth, especially in His ministry. New environments bring out the survivor in you, and they also challenge your response to newness. People identify new levels in themselves whenever they are placed in circumstances that are not conducive to live in, and they have to transform to live, so they do not die.

One of my favorite movies is Cast Away with Tom Hanks as the main character who is involved in a plane crash. He ends up on an island where he has to adapt to his new environment so he could stay alive.

Unexpected accidents happen for all of us, and we have to adapt to the change so that we can safeguard our survival. And on the other hand, they can serve a greater purpose in your lives. Perhaps it is to bring you into a closer relationship with God or give you the understanding that sometimes chaos is the best recipe to stir up the gifts in you. Choose to expose yourself to what can challenge you to become better. There is no magical formula to exposure. It has to be decided that you will not endorse mediocrity any longer. When you expose yourself to better, you appeal to your greater self. You owe it to yourself to discover all that God has placed in you.

The Holy Spirit Gives the Advantage

What an incredible opportunity the disciples had to walk with Jesus, God in the flesh. They had direct contact with His person, they knew

The Advantage of Now

the color of His eyes, and they were able to touch Him. But Jesus had to leave them because His time had come. Jesus says in John 16:7 (AMP), *"But I tell you the truth, it is to your advantage that I go away; for if I do not go away, the [a]Helper (Comforter, Advocate, Intercessor—Counselor, Strengthener, Standby) will not come to you; but if I go, I will send Him (the Holy Spirit) to you [to be in close fellowship with you]."*

The Spirit of God within you will illuminate your understanding regarding your timing on the earth. The Holy Spirit is the source; He is your inner power. He is your supernatural guide or your Paraclete, the one called alongside to help. A relationship with the Holy Spirit will always put you in proper time release sequence. No opportunity can pass you by; no door can close because the Holy Spirit is leading and guiding you.

The Holy Spirit dwells in you, giving you authority on the earth. Not only does the Holy Spirit remind you of our right standing with God, but He also reminds you of your new nature. He is the Spirit of Truth. (See John 16:13.) The Spirit of Truth dwells with you and in you to keep you in all your ways.

Satan is a created creature who wanted to be worshipped like God. That attitude led him to rebel against God in an attempt to establish his kingdom. Ultimately, Satan lost the battle. And what is most disastrous for Satan is that he lost his place. Because he knows he will never get his place back, he is an enemy of the believer. Lies are one of the primary weapons Satan uses; indeed, he is the father of lies. (See John 8:44.) A foundation built on lies is one that is always vulnerable to destruction; however, a foundation built on truth can stand the test of times. Anything that is a lie is a seed from Satan.

His job is to feed your mind the lie so it can prevent the manifestation of God's Word. A lie in every sense of the word is the total antithesis of truth. Lies bind, but truth liberates. Lies confuse, but truth brings clarity. Lies corrupt, but truth purifies. The Holy Spirit is sent to communicate truth that exposes all falsehood and error in your life while leading you into a closer relationship with Christ. When you submit to the Holy Spirit's guidance, you can embrace peace that comes with living in truth.

Jesus never claimed He was the source of power displayed through Him. His humanity was the means by which God showed His strength and willingness to use anyone who submitted themselves to Him. John 14:10 (NIV) says, *"Don't you believe that I am in the Father, and that the Father is in me? The words I say to you I do not speak on my own authority. Rather, it is the Father, living in me, who is doing his work."*

Jesus was the vessel by which God did the work, and through this example, faith is made possible. All of God (Spirit) was wrapped up in Jesus without measure, but Jesus's assignment was not to express His deity. Rather it was to express His humanity in submission to God's will. Jesus said, "It was the Father working in me," which means there were some inner dynamics taking place that was unseen by the world around Him.

There was chemistry between flesh and Spirit, but it began with the former submitting to the latter. As you read this, know that God is working in you, effectuating some things in you to bring about His plan. And you cannot base this operation off of your feelings because even when you don't feel Him working, He certainly is! You are His workmanship, created in Christ Jesus unto good works. (See Ephesians 2:10)

Just as God works through Christ, God desires to invade your inner reality with His power. Jesus's humanity was the channel through which God shows His willingness to use anyone who will submit themselves to Him. When the will of the flesh submits to the will of the Spirit, it activates the flow of revelation in a man's spirit, so man can now move in the world according to the mind of Christ. Galatians 5:17 (ESV) says, *"For the desires of the flesh are against the Spirit, and the desires of the Spirit are against the flesh, for these are opposed to each other, to keep you from doing the things you want to do."*

Deciphering God's will can be extraordinarily difficult for anyone who is seeking for their place in the world. We often get caught in the current of reality and lose sight of the spiritual goal to be like Christ.

The Advantage of Now

Spirit and flesh engage in an eternal battle of domination for the mind, the will, and, ultimately, the person.

It is impossible to blend your will with God's at any point in your life. It is either your will or His. There has to be a total denial of self for a total God takeover in your life. After all, the denial of self is the first prerequisite to taking up your cross and following Christ. Jesus said, *"the work you see me do is the Father working in me. Nothing I do is of my own accord, but I carry out the orders of heaven."* Jesus partnered with the invisible to manifest God's will on the earth. And if we are going to be effective, we must partner with the divine so that we can see results in our homes, our schools, our communities, and our country.

Be Deliberate

Be busy, but not just busy at just anything. Be busy at purpose, which means you seek to know your purpose for living and drive all of your energy in that direction. You will waste energy when you know what you must do, yet settle for what you are comfortable with doing.

In this life, we have to be busy with purpose on purpose, or we can get swallowed up in the tidal waves of changes and end up with the mentality of "I should have." This serves as a warning to many of us who are sluggishly living day by day without a goal in mind. Where are you aiming, and is your aim realistic? Aimlessness is a condition of indecision. With no destination or goal in mind, you can wander around your safe place for too long until you decide, enough is enough! God told Moses in Deuteronomy 2:3 KJV, *"You have compassed this mountain long enough, turn ye northward."* God is saying to you today, turn ye northward! It is time to go up into the fulfillment of your destiny, so pay attention to the mile markers in your life. Become consciously aware so that you do not miss what God has ordained for you to possess.

Practice the art of awareness. First, start noticing everything around you. In that, you will find clues as to where you are in your life right now. It may be seeing a billboard with a particular message, waiting at a stoplight while pedestrians cross by, or even looking out of a window while flying cross country. God hides His messages for you in the most obscure of places, and if you pay attention, that awareness can further propel you in the right direction.

Jesus Christ achieved perfect aim for you at Calvary, so we you it to yourself to point at the desired target and shoot your best shot. God expects that we aim and shoot straight into our destiny. Aim with deliberate purpose, and shoot with confidence.

I have seen many off-balance shots in the game of basketball that either made or changed history. Michael Jordan, for example, is the greatest to have ever played the game of basketball, yet even he made off-balance shots. When the points are tallied, and you come out in the win column, being off balance will not matter.

Off balance does not mean off your game. It only means that at that moment you must reassess, readjust and refine your posture. The question one would ask is, "Did you hit your mark?" God does not require perfection to meet destiny standards, but He needs faith. Believe in yourself, shoot your best shot now, and make the moment count.

You Have the Advantage

Having the advantage puts you one step closer to your victory.

—Ramon O. Gordon

With any advantage comes an opportunity to capitalize on something, especially if it is something bigger than you are. Serena Williams, tennis superstar, can tell us a little about having the advantage. In the game of tennis, the advantage is usually given to the player who scores the first point after deuce. He or she is placed in a better position to win the set because that last point gave them the advantage.

Our lives can, at times, mirror a tennis game. The effort and willpower produced from the last play will require the same energy, if not greater, to finish out the set. Just when you think you have spent enough in the last relationship, the college experience, or that marriage, you will then realize that more effort is required to secure the victory you so badly need. Which one of the plays of your life's experiences has given you the advantage? Perhaps you got the job you always wanted or maybe that financial bonus put you in a favorable position. Learn to capitalize on each action, so you do not lose that advantage. Your advantage has you postured for victory and much gain, and now is not the time to lose focus and grow weary. As dismal as the challenges seem, the circumstance is in your favor.

Having the advantage over something means to be put in a favorable or superior position because of a change in circumstance. We see sports teams who have the advantage all the time. Some emerge with a win; others come out with a defeat. You can lose the advantage in life because of many reasons. Maybe it is a lack of planning, loss of focus, or no exercise of faith. Whatever the reason is, you now must prepare your mind to use the advantage of all of life's lessons taught and learned for the advantage that comes with a new mindset.

Keep these three things in mind as you prepare for your next move:

1. Do not underestimate the challenge ahead. It is easy to adapt this "I got this" mentality when you are engaged in the pursuit of something meaningful. It is good to be confident, but it is important to be wise. *"Getting wisdom is the wisest thing you can do! And whatever else you do, develop good judgment"* (Proverbs 4:7 NLT). Failure can be a result of the haughtiness of a man's spirit, so to avoid this, we must take a careful approach to the challenges we face. Each challenge is uniquely different; therefore, we must take the right steps. Know why you are tackling that challenge. Are they for the right or wrong reasons? Are you fighting a losing battle? Once you know the truth to those questions, you can move forward with a clear head and heart.
2. Win from within. Seek to develop a healthy view of self as you position yourself for victory in any arena of life. You should know who you are and what you can take if you are going to take what God has ordained for you. Know your limits, strengths, and weaknesses. Once you know them, you build on that knowledge of the Word of God, and it becomes easy to resist what seeks to detour you from the path towards your destiny.
3. Dig deep. It is going to get ugly at times when you are focused, sometimes even unbearable. Your destiny is not going to

The Advantage of Now

come easily. There will be times when aborting the process seems easier than sticking it out. You will be forced to dig deep within to find the power within so that you can continue on your journey. Philippians 4:13 (AMP), *"I can do all things [which He has called me to do] through Him who strengthens and empowers me [to fulfill His purpose—I am self-sufficient in Christ's sufficiency; I am ready for anything and equal to anything through Him who infuses me with inner strength and confident peace.]"* Please know that you can only do what God has called you to do. Your assignment has an "All factor" tied to it. When you find your life's purpose, you find your "All factor". You were not meant to do everything, help everyone, write all the books, put on all the conferences. Your "All factor" is rooted in the call that is on your life, when you find your calling, live your life on full, and die empty.

Prepare for Action

"Therefore, preparing your minds for action, and being sober-minded, set your hope fully on the grace that will be brought to you at the revelation of Jesus Christ" (1 Peter 1:13 ESV).

Preparing our minds for action is not an easy task. There will be opposition and resistance as you shed your old mindset for a new one. Shedding that old mindset can mean removing some old friends, habits, or even a perspective of yourself. Once you know that you are the source of your unhappiness, you cannot live with that knowledge and be at peace. At some point, the reality of that truth prompts you to change. No longer can you live comfortably with the pattern of yesterday's failures, knowing there is another way, a better way.

Do not be fooled. Most of your inaction can be camouflaged in what you have associated yourself with: people, money, society, privileges, and so forth. The inundation of daily affairs and personal woes can stagnate you, but this cannot be an excuse to stay stuck. Comfort zones serve as a negative place rather than a positive. You are in a comfort zone when you are afraid of change and used to the familiar, or you find it hard to break away from a crippling routine of wandering and aimlessness.

So how do you move from stagnation to action? Understand that the condition of stagnation is a condition of the mind, first. The mind takes on a sort of mental rigor mortis and becomes fixed in mediocrity. Here are four steps to help overcome mental rigor mortis:

1. Read more. The more knowledge you ingest, the more you challenge your current knowledge base. Reading is the best way to stay current; expand your knowledge with subjects outside of your comfort level. Please understand that comfort is an enemy of your potential. Your circumstances want to convince you that you are capped off, but don't starve your potential because you are comfortable with a mode of learning. Go beyond that limitation, and when you feel you have exhausted yourself, go further.
2. Challenge your potential. Only you know your limitations, so never allow people to define that for you. Accept your challenge. Your potential is the untapped reality of who you are waiting to express itself in your outer reality. It is meant to be explored, not ignored. So if you have been ignored, it means you have decided to remain great within. Live on the level of what you put out. In other words, live on the level of your potential.
3. Keep pursuing your goals. A goal-oriented mind sets the pace for fulfillment. You give yourself a reason to live when you set goals.

On this journey toward self-fulfillment and growth, there will be times where we excel. And at times, we will feel uninspired, and we are stagnated. The awakening to action begins with a knowledge of your

The Advantage of Now

gifts and abilities because, through these, you will impact the world. God is so great that He gives gifts to all His children. Not one human being who has ever lived was born without something to offer. Even the precious child in her mother's womb has a gift that her creator has already downloaded in her.

Prep Time Is Over

Football in the south is like a religion. The bleachers, the smell, and the turf all play a part in the somewhat divine makeup of football. It is simply beloved. While I never played the sport, I have enjoyed watching it over the years. I can remember pep rallies in high school and the high energy associated with the team and school pride. Pep rallies were simply gatherings before a major sports event where young people cheer on their teams toward victory.

The pep rally was like a prep rally, and people geared their energy toward seeing their triumph over their football enemies. The pep rally was one thing, but the field was a different ballgame.

That same energy used in the auditorium must now be converted to strategy and skill on the field. Never get so caught up in the praise from the people in the auditorium that their silence affects you when you have caused a blunder on the field. Praise is fleeting, but purpose is steadfast. The auditorium here is your mind, and the field is your life. At times the translation from the mental to the physical can be difficult. However, this is where the battle is won, in the mind.

So, as you emerge from the auditorium of your life to the turf, shift gears into strategizing and planning your life's victory. Defeat on the field is a direct reflection of defeat in the auditorium. That moment of exhilaration and feeling of indestructibility vaporizes like smoke in the air when you step out into the reality of the challenge. You need huddle moments at times when life throws curveballs or when your last play draws a penalty. While the onlookers gawk at you, remember that who you have in your huddle truly matters. God is in your huddle, reading out your next play, and he is telling you to get open because He is about to throw you a pass that will put you in the victory column. So, you dropped the last pass, get open again! Prep time is over. The time is now to move into action. Take your position on the field of life.

Don't Listen to Them

According to John 12, Jesus enters Jerusalem for the last time before His crucifixion. He is greeted with an exuberant crowd, praising Him and shouting, *"Hosanna, blessed be the King of Israel."* It is important to note that, throughout all the praise and adoration, Jesus kept His composure. Learn to keep your composure during moments of praise because people can praise you today and put you down tomorrow.

In ancient middle eastern world, war leaders would ride warhorses in battle, but donkeys were ridden if they came in peace. The donkey was ridden by kings. Jesus rode in on a colt's ass; He sat high, bringing peace. Jesus riding into Jerusalem was not a sign of humility, but it was a mark of prestige. (See Zechariah 9:9-10). What He rode in on did not define Him. It simply transported Him closer to His destiny. What God has designed to transport you is not nearly as valuable as the place you are being transported to, so do not invest too much on the transport because it is only taking you to your exaltation. It does not matter what you are riding in on. It matters how you are positioned.

The Jews expected Jesus to ride in on a stallion and restore Israel back to political prominence. However, when Jesus left the auditorium of the heavenly places, He left with the mission to restore humanity back to God, not to tantalize the senses of the onlookers who had no desire to see the kingdom of God manifested.

Jesus knew He was the King of Israel and did not need endorsements from the Jerusalem times or the religious right to confirm His identity. He had already spent three years in ministry, and He was praised and ridiculed then. There was no need for Him to show another sign. Jesus was the sign that rode in on that spring day in Jerusalem, yet He kept His composure.

The Advantage of Now

Destiny minded people will hear the praise of man but filter it through his or her spirit because they know the source of their dependency. There was no need for Jesus to express His divinity at that moment because He knew where the source of His power lied. Like Jesus, you can be received by the praises of men only to come under siege with the words, "crucify him."

Remember these three things:

- **Know** who you are
- **Be** who you are
- **Show** who you are

"Comfort Normal"

Forward is the only direction God expects you to go, not backward. You have to decide to live your best life now. Sometimes living the best life means leaving the worst places of our life. That failure, that abuse, or those bad choices can define your future, if you let it. There are no advantages to be gained when we settle in the comfort of our existence. Therein lies the disadvantage. The temporary plushness of your comfort zone only serves for a time before that *Kairos* moment challenges your normal. A sense of destiny will challenge you to action, and you will have to muster up the courage to follow that instinct to live out your purpose.

To produce effectively, you have to view comfortability as your enemy. Anything that does not challenge you or anything that praises your mediocrities are enemies of your destiny. You cannot ride mediocrity to success. Respond to the truth that you cannot produce effectively when you are comfortable. Most times the best of you can only be found outside of what I call your "comfort normal." These are places where our comfort zones become our normal experience. The icy dispositions of apathy and lethargy will quench the zest for life and the thrilling pursuit of purpose if you choose to remain in your comfort normal.

Ramon O. Gordon

You see, I am terrified of spending a great deal of my life too comfortable! At the end of my life, I do not want to have the tragic reality of pondering the what-ifs. God does not want you to live in the what-ifs, He wants you to live in the what-is. For some people it's not that agonizing to ponder because they have decided to allow life's circumstances to decide the path in which they tread. But there are those who know God has more in store, who must break from the grip of complacency, into the conviction of personal accountability.

Often our "comfort normal" is just camouflaged laziness. Over time, it becomes easy to adapt to laziness without holding any accountability for yourself. This is where you can experience silent frustration. But this is the time to be occupied with your destiny moves, not excuses. With the gifts and talents that God has given you, something should always be on the agenda. Your comfort normal can house toxic character defects that can stunt your growth toward destiny fulfillment. Even if you have never been locked behind steel bars, the irony is that you can be free yet remain locked behind the steel bars of your comfort normal.

It's time to emerge from your comfort zone into the challenge that your destiny can only bring. Observing the view from your steel bars is not enough at this point in your life. Break out! Only then can you go through the process that leads to greatness. So how do you do this? Love discomfort!!

I had a brief stent with American Tae Kwon Do a while ago- Bruce Lee has always been an enigmatic figure in my mind, simply amazing human being. As I did my warm-ups in class one evening, my instructor had us do hamstring stretches, and it was debilitating! I can still hear him saying, *"If you feel the pain, then you know it's working. Come on, thirty more seconds."* You see, the moment where the pain seemed so intense was the exact moment that transformation was taking place in my body. Your transformation only takes place in the discomfort of those moments when the pain seems unbearable.

Hurts for a Reason

Nothing great is ever achieved in comfort. Even the mother who gives birth to the child does not do so in comfort, but rather in discomfort. Nothing is ever achieved in comfortable situations, and if it were, it would be easy to abandon. It is shocking even painful to hear of mothers who abandon their babies in alleys after they are born. They invested the pain but lacked the courage to go through the process of raising a baby. Once you have sacrificed and endured the steps to achieve success, letting go will not be so easy. Pain is only invested by those who have the long-term in mind, not for those who just seek the thrill of momentary gratification. To birth what is new, you have to be willing to endure the temporary discomfort of pain until you can hold the promises of God in your hands. In other words, never let the pain of the moment outlive the pleasure of the promise.

> John 16:21 (ESV) says, *"When a woman is giving birth, she has sorrow because her hour has come, but when she has delivered the baby, she no longer remembers the anguish, for joy that a human being has been born into the world."*

Sometimes you have to go through the pain of regret, rejection, guilt, and bad choices to come into a better you. You may ask, "Does it require all of this?" Yes, it does. Always remember that there is a better you in you and every trial you encounter is transforming you into a better person. For every person who goes to the gym often, the pain you feel in the morning is a sign that the muscles worked out the night before are coming into form. The testing and trials in your life have the same effect, and when you can wake up the morning after the worst night of your life and still find joy, peace, and an unwavering allegiance to your vision, your testing is working in your favor!

The pain it takes to achieve your goals is more bearable than the agony that comes from living the rest of life with regret. Pain is included in the process to achieving your goals. It is an inevitable part of the journey. You see, pain is the motivator that guarantees results. The pain of discipline safeguards the pleasure of reward.

Oftentimes we experience the reality of what is and not the reality of what was. We are the benefactors of the works of great men. We can go to Egypt and enjoy the awesome view of the pyramids or go to China and view the extravagance of the Great Wall. Or we could even go to the White House and explore its deep history, but there is another side to the reality of what we see. That pain is rooted in the reality of men moving limestone in Egypt, men gathering brick and mortar for miles in China, and slaves laying bricks in Washington DC. The process that your destiny has you on will produce pain, but the pain will carve out a place for you in history.

You will achieve your dreams but not before pain. Do not allow pain to disrupt your progress, but use it as a reminder that what you fought for—and are now fighting for—was worth it all.

The Cross of Christ

People who take part with you in your elevation do not always participate with you in the pain it took to get to your elevation. Actually, the higher you ascend, the greater the pain is. Jesus says, *"Take up your cross daily and follow me."* (See Luke 9:23 KJV.) The call from that text is to participate in self-sacrifice and humility. Jesus carried His cross, and He was elevated on that cross to be seen by all men. The cross you carry in your life will be the tool used for your elevation. Jesus' ascension on the cross was not to benefit Him, it was to benefit everyone who would look in His direction. Do not believe for a moment that your ascension is a rise to fame and riches in the kingdom of God because it is not. God has risen you up to be a witness of His saving power and grace.

Jesus endured pain on the cross, but the pain did not defeat His Spirit. Ultimately, He would secure man's eternal victory, snatch back our authority from Satan, reposition man back in a place of dominance,

The Advantage of Now

and break the curse of sin over the lives of anyone who would believe in His finished works. What an amazing sacrifice!

Jesus gives us the advantage so we would become all we were created to be. That creativity in you, that greatness in you, is waiting for you to use your pain as a source of power and not an excuse for inaction and fear. It is time to get over some of the psychological wear and tear and ego defenses and claim our future with confidence. Blaming someone for not being what you needed them to be at one point in your life is pointless because it is our responsibility to make our lives work. The Son of God endured the temporary horrors of pain just to secure the eternal splendor of a name that is above every name, Jesus Christ.

Jesus stayed on the cross long enough to achieve total victory for all mankind, but He didn't stay there forever. The cross was only a temporary place, yet this tool gave Jesus total victory. Not only do we celebrate this victory from the periphery, but we are also partakers of this victory by faith. Jesus had a vantage point while hanging on that cross and could see the impact His sacrifice would make on mankind. You may be missing tremendous opportunities because you see your advantage as a handicap. View it not as a handicap but as a perspective. You are required to see the advantage even in the most uncomfortable of situations which will give you an exclusive view into what God has for you.

Know your advantage even when the vicissitudes of life try to redirect you away from your vision. Your current place or position in life may not be as bad as you think it is. It just requires that you assess it differently. Knowing your advantage gives you another perspective and a new set of lenses so you can see in and through the circumstance.

Your Move

To truly experience the deep, you have to get off the shore of your life into the depths of your potential.
—Ramon O. Gordon

This chapter is designed to teach us how to move in sync with God's Word. Instruction is crucial in our quest toward fulfilling the purposes of God in our lives. Not hearing correctly can lead us into a web of confusion and mental entanglement, therefore instruction is necessary at every level of life, whether it is a toddler, adolescent, or fully grown adult. When we fail to listen to wise advice, we can suffer the consequences later in life. There is a time to make a move on what God has placed on your heart because He has orchestrated your life to go according to His will. It is for you to grasp it in time and move on it with conviction.

According to the Gospel of Luke chapter five, the disciples had been fishing all night and caught nothing but Jesus gave them specific instructions to change their position. One move can alter the rest of your life forever. One decision to learn, to overcome, to grow, can shift the dynamics of your life forever. The Sea of Galilee was known then for its wide selection of fish, and it boasted at least eighteen different species at that time. So, a lack of fish was not the problem, a lack of positioning was the issue. It is not that there is not enough out there

The Advantage of Now

for everybody. The problem is that we have not been taught to position ourselves for success.

Positioning is critical to the process of obedience in life. The term "position" is an active verb. It means to arrange something or put someone or something in place. A change of position will place you in a greater posture to receive God's blessings. It is strategic positioning! According to the scriptures, the fishermen toiled all night and caught nothing. I am not sure why the fishermen did not catch any fish because they were qualified and skilled. But for them to be in a greater posture to receive the biggest catch of their lives, they had to move at Jesus's command. They had to change their position. You need to know four steps in preparation for the biggest catch of your life.

1. Posture Yourself

I alluded to a few points earlier about posturing and how critical it is to receiving God's blessings. I want to further elaborate on that point. As a young father, I have seen my baby girl grow so fast. I remember feeding her one day, but she kept rejecting the bottle. She spit up a few times as well. I could not understand why she kept spitting up until my wife told me she was not in the correct posture. The bottle was warm, the cloth was in place, but she was not in the right posture, so she kept spitting up nutrients that would be beneficial to her growth.

Just like my daughter, many of us have been in position to receive but in the wrong posture. We have allowed people to position us in various places in our lives, and we have missed out on God's promises. How many words have you received from God that did not reach your spiritual digestive system because you were not in the right posture? You can be postured and positioned for success in the wrong business, job, or even relationship. That is why knowing who you are is very critical to taking advantage of the times and not wasting hours and minutes in the wrong place. You cannot fully stretch into who God has created you to be when you are planted in the wrong place.

In human anatomy, the body that does not have good posture can result in long-term defects. Yes, bad posture can impact your health and happiness, and the same idea applies to the Spirit. Your spiritual health and happiness can be affected if careful attention is not given to making necessary changes.

Hebrews 12:1 (KJV) says, *"Therefore, seeing we also are compassed about with so great a cloud of witnesses, let us lay aside every weight, and the sin which doth so easily beset us, and let us run with patience the race that is set before us."*

The writer of the book of Hebrews makes the point in the above text that we should shed ourselves of unnecessary weight so our progress will not be stagnated. The words lay aside in Hebrews 12:1 is the Greek word *apotithimi*. This word is a compound word, *apo*, which means away, and *tithimi* means to place or lay something down. The imagery here is casting something aside and pushing it as far away as possible. Like taking off garments, this is how we ought to lay aside those things that have negatively affected our walk with God. The action is deliberate and it requires the power of God's Spirit. You must decide that there are some things that you will not wear any longer. Decide each morning you wake up; I will not wear fear, I will not wear anger, I will not wear regret. Cast away the garments that remind you of your past life so that you can embrace the positive future that God has for you in Christ.

Every one of us has a sin that doth so easily beset, and it takes the power of the Holy Spirit to help us overcome that particular struggle. Unnecessary weight can contribute to slothfulness and a discontent for life resulting in an inability to run efficiently. After all, you cannot run with extra weight. It hides your true form and restricts your God-given potential. Get rid of the weight that keeps you out of great spiritual form so you can continue running the race. Sin is excess. It likes to normalize itself in our everyday life leaving us indifferent to the convicting power of the Holy Spirit. God has given us power over besetting sins. It is not meant for our sin to decide our pace because Christ is our pacesetter. He sets the course, marks out the path, and all we do is follow Him.

2. Listen to Instruction

Proverbs 19:20 AMP says, "Listen to counsel, receive instruction, *and* accept correction, that you may be wise in the time to come." And Proverbs 8:10 AMP says, *"Take my instruction rather than [seeking] silver, and take knowledge rather than choicest gold."* I say, "Listen today so you will not regret tomorrow."

These two scriptures embody the importance of hearing and receiving instruction, and as believers, we must adopt an attitude that is quick to hear and slow to speak. There are short- and long-term effects of hearing instructions, which can prove to be fatal to anyone who has no honor in hearing. Following and listening to instruction is a skill that has to be mastered. Leonardo Da Vinci once quipped, "Most people listen without hearing."

To truly listen, one must be focused. It requires focus to employ the principles that are being heard. Learn to listen without confusing what you hear with your own motives. Discernment is required here. Listen today so you will not regret tomorrow. What I allow my mind to meditate on today becomes the soil by which I build my future on tomorrow

This is what God told Joshua to do in the Old Testament. He told him to meditate on the book of the law because by doing so he would prosper and have good success. (See Joshua 1:8.) There is a correlation between meditation and success. You see, meditation is the filter between the Spirit world and your heart. The cure for a clean heart is meditating on the right thoughts. When positive thoughts get in, negative thoughts must find a way out! Success is the by-product of the force of focus. Simply put, you cannot be a truly focused individual and not know success. If your focus is right, you will find true success.

Some situations we face are designed to teach us how to listen to God. There are seasons where all we can do is listen for our next move; then there are seasons where God expects us to act on His Word. The disciples were at a place where they were not productive, and they were caught up in the system of that day. However, the instructions of Christ positioned them for greater.

How long have you been at the place of normalcy and routine, longing for satisfaction? How long have you settled in a place that you have now outgrown? Be honest with yourself today, and embrace the challenge of taking heed to God's voice so you can be in the position to make the biggest catch of your life.

3. Evaluate Before You Launch

Evaluate where you are before launching out to where you should be. After you have evaluated your situation, you are in a better position to make the necessary changes. There has to be a time where reevaluation takes place so changes can be made. Even gazelles on the African plain only graze in green pasture for a brief time until what they have been feeding on dries up. They are soon looking for greener pasture, so they ensure their survival. Their need for nourishment was in the other place. Are you trying to feed yourself on dry seasons? Even the manna that God fed the children of Israel with dried up. Perhaps God is bringing you into a new season, and what sustained you in the old season is not necessary for the new. Shift with your inner hunger for continued growth, personal success, and total fulfillment.

Anything that remains in the same place too long becomes common, and once it becomes common, it loses its uniqueness. You are too unique to continue blending in with your environment. You are too full of potential to continue assuming the position but never catching anything. Simon and the fishermen assumed the position, they were poised to receive but caught nothing. Posture has nothing to do with success- you can look the part and not be the part, all at the same time. Therefore, we need the Holy Spirit to help us translate posture into production. Not only will you look like you are successful, you will produce the fruits of success because you are sensitive to the voice of God.

When Jesus saw the disciples, He wanted to change their posture from expectancy to manifestation. However, for there to be manifestation, the disciples had to listen to His instructions. The season for catching nothing is over. You are too full of God to continue coming up empty-handed. There is a tidal wave of

The Advantage of Now

opportunities coming into your life and you must reposition yourself to see a breakthrough. You can only do this by taking the initiative to launch out.

4. Launch Out

Luke 5:4 (KJV) says, *"Now when he had left speaking, he said unto Simon, launch out into the deep, and let down your nets."* Jesus gave the disciples a command to go further into the deep and drop their nets. His instructions were a directive marked with two steps. Launch out, and let down. The word "launch" in this text is a nautical term, and it means to put out to sea or to bring up or back. Jesus related to them by speaking their language first, and then He gave them instruction. Jesus is always relatable to your situation; He can feel everything you go through. But it is important to consider that Jesus may find you in a stagnant place, but He will challenge you to move to a greater location. In other words, Jesus was saying to the fishermen, "Do not stay here and waste your time and energy in a place where you have been toiling all night."

The message is to those who have exerted all resources, intellect, and loyalty on something that has not produced anything. Stop toiling. To toil literally means to labor. The Greek meaning for toil is *a strike that is so hard, it literally weakens or debilitates; deep fatigue.* Are you striking continuously in effort at a place that can no longer produce? If so, Jesus is calling you from toil to rest. When you enter God's rest you will see an abundance of blessings released in your life that He has already prepared for you. To achieve your full potential, you must obey the voice of the Lord and go to the place He has instructed you to go. Launch out into the deep! Accept the challenge that your gift and talent bring, and through the power of the Holy Spirit, you will be able to manifest God's works on the earth.

Many times we settle in where we fit in, which yields little to no results, and we stay ignorant of the possibilities that come with launching out in the deep. Do not allow yourself to settle in shallow places, but take heed to God's voice as He directs your life into greater fulfillment.

Unfamiliar Places Shatter Old Expectations

Some of your expectations must be shattered before you can launch into new places. The job that hired you with a promise of a great future downsizes and leaves you jobless, or what started as a loving marriage ends up in the divorce court. We all have experienced shattered expectations, but just because you have experienced broken expectations does not mean you should never expect again. A healthy expectation will help you to form projections of where you want your vision to go, the people you want to work with, and the results you want to see.

Everyone who launches with you will not stay with you. What you have changed positions to catch will be misunderstood by people in your circle. Everyone cannot handle your load, and if you beg people to go where you are heading, you make them a handicap in your process. You need the right people around you who will help you when the load is too heavy. The disciples did not have time to invite anyone on board. They had to move on the words of Jesus.

In case you were waiting for others to join the ship of your destiny, you may miss your moment. Now is not the time to wait for folks who want to get on your ship. Those people are opportunists who only want to connect to you because of where you are going, but only on their time. For where you are going next, God wants to bring you there fresh without the baggage of your past failures as well as the baggage of others' opinions. Your ship has already set sail, allow the winds to carry you to your place of abundance.

Deep Longing for a Fulfilled Place

Psalm 42:7 (KJV) says, *"Deep calleth unto deep at the noise of thy waterspouts: all thy waves and billows are gone over me.*

God desires to fellowship with you, all of you, and it summons the deep places within you. That deep thing in you is the place where you are fed up with living a mundane, routine life, absent of God's presence and blessings. Have you ever been frustrated about anything that absorbed the energy needed to live a productive life? It is a frustration that comes from your potential rather than your incompetence. It is not that you cannot do it. But there is this feeling of inadequacy, a sense you are not good enough. You are adequate! God would not have equipped you with the tools, the talent, and the charisma if you were not adequate to the task.

Time is too short to settle in a place and not catch anything, as those fishermen did. Whether it is a relationship or a job, settling suppresses your potential. Let God pull you from:

- the depths of ignorance to the heights of revelation knowledge;
- the failures of the past to the brightness of an empowered future;
- the shallowness of yesterday's blame to the promises of tomorrow's accountability; and
- the dependency of others to the realization of your true potential.

Wait: Mastering Patience

> James 1:4 (KJV) says, *"But let patience have her perfect work, that you may be perfect and entire, wanting nothing."*

That word "patience" in this text is *hupomone* in the Greek language, and it means an abiding under, it is patience that grows under trial, and it not easily dismissed when the process gets difficult. When you are patient you will not abort your vision prematurely because it seems unreachable, but you will remain steadfast in your pursuit. This patience is opposed to a defeatist mentality, and it forges a bond between the believer and the fulfillment of the promise. It is very critical to develop an attitude of patience during the process so that, when things do not go the way you envisioned, you will not be easily discouraged. At times, the vision seems like it is in another stratosphere, and the day-to-day rigor of working on it can weaken your faith. But if you keep working at it, you will see it come to pass. *"The night cometh when no man can work"* (James 9:4 KJV).

Keep in mind that you continue to fail if you are not continuously engaged in the fulfillment of your vision. So continue to work while it is day so the night can be a testament of the conscious efforts toward success made while it was day.

The problem with the waiting process is that many of us remain inactive when we should be actively moving to fulfill our destiny on the earth. The waiting process should involve your entire being. Your will, intellect, and mind should all be engaged in the pursuit of your life's goals. That word "wait" as a noun has two meanings according to audioenglish. org. The first meaning notes that waiting is a time during which some action is awaited. Second, it is the act of waiting. As a verb, the word "wait" means to stay in one place and anticipate or expect something, to wait before acting, or to look forward to the probable occurrence of a thing.

There is no probable occurrence in the mind of God; there is only completion in the mind of God. To suggest there was a probable occurrence in the mind of God is to suggest there is a defect in God's providence. Not so! Jesus Christ was in the mind of God as the Lamb slain from the foundation of the world. Before God speaks, it is already done. Before He thinks it, it has already come into existence. Because God's agenda for your life is already complete, your faith to act today will move you forward into what God has predestined for your life.

Find Something to Do

> Ecclesiastes 9:10 (NLT) says, *"Whatever you do, do well. For when you go to the grave, there will be no work or planning or knowledge or wisdom."*

The scripture is saying that when you find your calling, invest all of yourself completely, and do it to the best of your ability. You see, we often wait on God to make the next move when He has already completed His plan for our lives, so stop waiting for someday and make today the day that you take control of your life. You are a vessel for God, a conduit. Like the flow of electricity through wires, God has chosen to flow through your life. Psalm 27:14 (KJV) says, *"Wait on the Lord, be of good courage, and he will strengthen thine heart: wait, I say, on the Lord."*

This scripture is not just saying to us that we should just sit back and let God do everything. God has already done what He is going to do. It is up to you to declare words of faith over your life and move ahead with determination. The scripture suggests that, while I wait, I bind together, collect, and expect something to come. Get twisted up in the fulfillment of your vision, and place your attention in a certain direction with an expectant attitude. You can avoid the devastating blows of inaction later if you take time to invest in your dream today and what your dream needs is careful attention to what must be done today to guarantee long-lasting fulfillment.

Let Down Your Nets

Everyone knows that, in the world of culinary arts or your grandmother's kitchen, certain foods taste better when soaked in seasoning overnight. This practice allows the seasoning to settle in the meat so the flavor can make its way to the bone. When Jesus told Peter to launch out and let down the nets, initially he thought about it, but he eventually obeyed the Lord's instructions. Like the culinary experience, some of the seasons of life are designed to teach growth in character.

Please do not misunderstand me here. I am not speaking of settling in a negative sense, but a positive one. At times you will learn positive lessons through negative experiences. Some people settle for the negativity that thrives in certain relationships, jobs, or even people, because events in their history have had a negative impact on their self-esteem. But when you know who and whose you are, you will reject the mind-set that you are weak and deprived of confidence. Jesus tells us in the text that we should settle where He has placed us, not where we have situated ourselves. Where you have ended up may be a result of the navigation of your own will yet God can use that place to reveal His next plan for your life. You did not get away from God; you ended up right where He wanted you to be. The problem with settling where we place ourselves is that our knowledge is limited and we are more programmed by our carnal nature to move out of emotion than by the leading of the Holy Spirit.

It is possible to miss out on what God has ordained for you when you are hasty to move from a place that God told you to settle in. Launch out into the deep (place), and let down your nets (settle). Jesus picked the place, and all Simon had to do was go there. I believe that God is speaking to somebody right now as he or she reads this! God is saying to you that He has already prepared a place for you, but you are to settle in the place of the promise so you can reap a harvest. Get to the place, drop your nets, settle in that location, and prepare to receive a catch that is going to position you for increase in all areas of your life and for the rest of your life.

Pull It In

Jesus told Simon to *"let down your nets for a draught."* In other words, Jesus told Simon, "This is the place where you will see a miracle, so let down your nets." The catch is guaranteed, but only through obedience. The disciples did nothing new in the place Christ instructed them to go. They used the same fishing protocol, same net, just in a new place. Often it is not the tools that are defected, rather it may simply be a defected willpower to fight what been normalized in your life. Maybe you have the right tools but you are in the wrong company, or you have the right tools, but the wrong business plan. Strategies do not have to change for progress to be made. Some draughts in your life is not fueled by your incompetence; sometimes it is a lack of faith in God's word.

The Advantage of Now

Luke 5:6–7 (KJV) says, *"And when they had done this, they enclosed a great multitude of fishes: and their net brake. And they beckoned unto their partners, which were in the other ship, that they should come and help them. And they came, and filled both the ships, so that they began to sink."*

When they had done what? When they obeyed the command of Jesus, they were put in position to pull in a big catch. They caught so much that their net began to break. When you are obedient to the Word of God, your latter end will always be better than the former because God's Word will place you right where you need to be so you can reap the blessings that He has prepared for you. The breakthrough you seek is just waiting on your repositioning; get to that place, and you will see an abundance. Obedience always positions you for the blessings, while disobedience keeps you confined to a stagnant place. Your blessing is always in the place of obedience. Total trust in God's Word will release you into a season of unlimited provision for your life.

First Corinthians 2:9 (KJV) reads, *"But as it is written, Eye hath not seen, nor ear heard, neither have entered into the heart of man, the things which God hath prepared for them that love him."*

God has prepared things for you. Things! That means that God has already prepared everything that you and I will ever receive. They are not being prepared; God is not getting them ready. They are already in place in the Spirit. How do we get access to the things that God has prepared for us? Faith! God responds to two things: faith and obedience.

That word "things" implies that God has reserved for you far more than what you think is yours. Faith will break through the limitation of the natural to release the abundance of the supernatural. Go get your things! Only God knows what rightfully belongs to you, and many times we live our lives waiting for a man to do what only God can. I must add that even miracles require some human effort because with divine accomplishment comes human effort. If the disciples felt the tug in their net but did not apply effort to pull that net up, they would have missed the miracle. Are you asking God for a miracle? If that is the case, be ready to listen to His instructions. Only then will you reap the benefits of your obedience to God's word.

It Begins with a Dream

What happens to a dream deferred? Does it dry up like a raisin in the sun? Or does it explode?
—Langston Hughes

Dr. King's "I Have a Dream" speech set a current in motion for equality and justice for all people in this country. Some people suggest that this aspect of his dream is not fully realized but has made considerable progress in the right direction. Regardless, the truth is that Dr. King was not the only one dreaming on August 28, 1963, but many boys and girls, men and women, whites and blacks, and people from all diverse backgrounds were dreaming that day. Dr. King's dream set in motion a pursuit for unity and equality, and although we have a long way to go, progress has been made.

Whether you echo your dream in front of millions or speak it in the quietness of your car garage, it's still a dream. That is where the dream begins, in the quiet incubators of life's experiences, just waiting for the right moment to burst free. Dreams give humanity the advantage to choose love, peace, optimism, everything that is good in life. But humanity must dream, or we will continue to see the godlessness, corruption, poverty, and disease choke the life out of this and future generations. A dream gives hope and encourages optimism. It is the right of anybody who dares to believe, regardless of his or her status in life.

What is a dream? It is a guideline or blueprint for your life. If you have seen something in a dream, it is attainable because, if you can see it, you can have it. This is why the scriptures tell us to walk by faith and not by sight. (See 2 Corinthians 5:7.) Faith fuels the dream, while sight contradicts what you see in your spirit.

There is always a contradiction between sight and faith. Faith pulls from God, while sight pulls from facts. Your dream needs your faith to come into agreement in time so that faith will help bring your dream to pass on the earth; I will deal more extensively on faith in chapter six. Your dream has the potential to be ageless and impose profound influence on future generations. But those individuals will not reap the benefits of your dream if you remain a sleep dreamer.

According to Wikipedia, dreams are successions of images, ideas, emotions, and sensations that occur subconsciously in the mind during certain stages of sleep. It goes on to say that dreams occur during rapid eye movements (REM) during sleep. Now I know that these theories hold true to many in the science world. But I want to coin the term "sleep dreamers."

In my world, sleep dreamers live with a dream mindset but lack the courage to live out their dream. They live in a sedated state of dream realization, and they passively pursue that dream but actively live in what is convenient at that moment. God does not just want His children to dream passively. He wants us to carry out the dream with courage actively. Only an active pursuit of what God has shown you will bring fulfillment to your life.

The Courageous Dreamer

Dreamers must be courageous in pursuit of their dreams and aspirations. Have the courage to live your dream the way God has revealed it to you. Your dream is tailor-made to fit you and no one else. Therefore living someone else's dream will never work for you. It does not matter how attractive and scenic that person's life may seem. Trying to emulate their dream will only lead to frustration.

The Advantage of Now

God spoke to Joshua in the Old Testament as he prepared to march the children of Israel into the Promised Land, and told him to be strong and of good courage. This task came upon Joshua after Moses's sudden death. Joshua was already prepared to lead because of his front row seat in Moses's administration as well. Moses laid his hand on him as a sign of transferal of authority and power. The only thing that God required of Joshua was that he be strong and courageous.

And this is what God requires of you who is in pursuit of your dreams- to be strong and courageous. A lack of courage will severely damage your chances at achieving anything in life, and this can lead to an unfulfilled life. Courage is the ability to do something that frightens you. It stems from your potential or innate ability to do. Courage is the actual acting out of your potential. It is instinctive and is always revealed in awkward or unplanned moments.

You did not know you were a good orator until you were put on the spot during a session at work or at that conference. You did not know you were a competent musician until you sat down at that piano and struck a few keys. You did not know you could run an entire organization until your boss put you in charge for the week.

You see, you did not know until you were placed in a demanding situation. Whatever the circumstances were, it revealed an aspect of your potential that you did not know existed. Please understand with me that, just because that ability or gift is lying dormant in you, it does not mean that it was never there. One definition of "dormant" is alive but not growing. It is a period where growth and development have been temporarily stopped. You can only grow so much before that place becomes tight and you now need to change your position so you can expand. Your thoughts and ideas need room to explore and breathe in new arenas of discoveries.

Oftentimes many of us frighten ourselves when we do something that we never knew we had the power to do. Again, this is not because that potential never existed, but perhaps it laid dormant because of unbelief. You came into this world prepackaged and ready for use. Dreamers must believe in themselves if they are going to pull from their greatness reservoirs. Your dream demands that you be courageous and secure the steps to see it fulfilled.

It takes courage for,

- a young man to overcome the tentacles of poverty, abuse, and a broken home to find success and achievement;
- a young woman who has been a victim of rape and exploitation to take control of her life regardless of everything she has been through; or
- someone with a vision to start a company after being fired from a job.

Joseph in You

Joseph represents all of us who have ever dreamed against the odds and had to go through the process to see fulfillment. Like Joseph, many of us have seen the future God has prepared for us through our dreams. Friends, your dream is your guide to living the life that God has designed for you. It is your compass that points towards a destination. A dream guided Joseph's life on the earth, and your dream will guide you on your earthly experience.

Joseph had a dream. The Hebrew word for "had a dream" means "to bind firmly." Joseph became bound up in the dream that God gave him; he got twisted up in what God showed him. The beginning for every dream bearer is to get twisted up in the dream that God has revealed. Once that sense of purpose consumes you, you begin to act, think, and even speak differently. Your sense of direction is like a dog picking up a scent. Hound dogs hunt by scent rather than sight. It is remarkable that their sense of smell takes them directly to what they are hunting.

Like the hound dog, sometimes we have to rely not on what we can see but on what we believe. In some way, faith is that scent we have to sniff out as we navigate through our life circumstances. What Joseph saw was so intense and so real that it had him instantly. Does

The Advantage of Now

your dream have you? Because if it does, you will know it. It becomes almost impossible to become unstuck to what God has bound you to. Joseph's dream was in his spirit. The first dream awakened his consciousness, but the second confirmed it. Until the dream has you, you have not dreamed of greatness yet.

Your Mouth Is the Key

A closed mouth is a closed destiny.

—Delroy Smith

The key to realizing dream fulfillment is understanding what and when to speak. Our mouths are tools by which our words create our reality. After Joseph had spoken the dream to his brethren, this is what their assessment was, *"And his brethren said to him, shall thou indeed reign over us? Or shall thou indeed have dominion over us? And they hated him yet the more for his dreams, and for his words"* (Genesis 37:8 KJV).

Do you see this? They hated him for his dream first, and then they detested him for his words. Not only did the content of his dream offend them, what he spoke affronted them more. Remember, dreams are unspoken realities of a man's spirit, and the only way for the dream to find an outlet is for it to be spoken. It was not until Joseph spoke that he was immediately placed on the path of dream realization.

When God gives you a dream, the first thing you do is speak. Naturally, the initial thing people do is keep it in because the dream's content can even be startling to the dreamer. What you see yourself becoming may not necessarily reflect what you are and where you are right now. But your dream never reveals your actual self; it always reveals your potential self. The more startling the dream is, the more it may suggest that God had to give it. Not only once did Joseph speak, but twice. Your dream changes your language; your language can change your life.

In Genesis, we see God using His words to form the world. There are a series of "Let there be" statements in Genesis chapter one. God's

Word set the course of creation in motion, and everything that God spoke to had to come into manifestation. I want you to consider that we have the same power with our words. God blew His Spirit into man and gave man the same creative abilities that He possesses. (See Genesis 2:7.)

Yes, my friends! We can use our words to carve out our destiny, heal our marriages, bless our children, and even curse our lives! Your mouth is the gateway for your vision, persecution, and triumph. When you do not speak, you delay your dream realization process. Your mouth gives feet to your dream. If you want to see your dream gain traction in the earth, start speaking! Joseph's greatest tool was his mouth. His dream was the resource that was looking for an outlet.

The Bible says in Genesis 37:7 NIV, *"We were binding sheaves of grain out in the field when suddenly my sheaf rose and stood upright, while your sheaves gathered around mine and bowed down to it."* Joseph dreamed a dream and told it to his brothers, not once but twice. Genesis 37:9, *"And he dreamed yet another dream, and told it his brethren, and said, Behold, I have dreamed a dream more; and, behold, the sun and the moon and the eleven stars made obeisance to me."* Each dream portrayed Joseph in the position of power and influence and depicted his family paying him homage. The dreams troubled his family. There was no need for any interpretation. "What are you insinuating, Joseph? Will we bow down to you and serve you?" His brothers were enraged at the mere recital of his dreams.

However, Joseph's dreams go beyond him and point to Jesus Christ. We will see the importance of Christ as God would give His Son absolute supremacy. Jesus Christ would be exalted, that at the name of Jesus every knee should bow, of things in heaven, and things in earth, and things under the earth. (See Philippians 2:7)

We often say we should be careful about who we tell our dreams to, but I firmly believe, if Joseph had not told his dream, its fulfillment would have been delayed. Every dreamer has a process, and Joseph's was never activated until he told his dream. Your mouth is the key to activating the process of dream realization. Death and life are

The Advantage of Now

in the power of the tongue so what you speak can give life or bring death. The mouth is the tool that brings you into covenant with the promises of God. When you speak, you openly declare the will of God for your life. When you speak, you give eternity permission to move on your behalf.

Joseph's mouth activated his dream, and your mouth is the key to activating the dream God has given you. So be mindful of what you speak because your words can either halt or propel the process of fulfilling the promise. Your dream needs an outlet, which is your mouth. Do not be afraid to speak what God has placed in your spirit.

Your Action, Their Response, and Your Benefit

The scripture shows us the upward trajectory that Joseph's dream catapulted him into; not only does the dream consume him, the dream sets him in motion. *"And they said one to another, behold, this dreamer cometh"* (Genesis 37:19 KJV). Dreamers are always in motion. They explore the world around them, seek out opportunities, and live unapologetically. Dreamers are always engaged in something that is productive. They do not have time to gossip and envy the other person's success.

Your dream will give you new lenses forcing you to see yourself and the world in different light. The dream will awaken your curiosity, and you will ask, "is this possible?" When these questions begin to surface, you will know that your dream has consumed you. It is always when you are in active pursuit of dream realization that you encounter the hatred and spitefulness of the people around you. Why? As long as you remain a sleep dreamer, your inner circle likes you, but as soon as you rise from inaction and pursue your goals, you become a target for their negativity.

The first dream awakened Joseph's appetite for destiny; the second only confirmed it. And after that, the only thing left for him to do was start moving. *"Behold, this dreamer cometh"* should be the highlight for the rest of your life. Become so consumed by what God has shown you that you will stop at nothing until you see your dream fulfilled.

My friends, God has set you on an unstoppable path to victory. Hold up your head and receive your position of favor. Joseph was the son of Israel's old age, so he stole the affection and love of his father. So Israel made Joseph a coat of many colors. Genesis 37:3-4 AMP, *"now Israel (Jacob) loved Joseph more than all his children, because he was the son of his old age; and he made him a [distinctive] multi-colored tunic. 4 His brothers saw that their father loved Joseph more than all of his brothers; so they hated him and could not [find it within themselves to] speak to him on friendly terms."*

The coat identified him with man, but the dream acknowledged him with God. Joseph's coat was his biblical-day label, much like our modern-day labels today. If you are not careful, you can allow what people put on you to become the identity they use to recognize you. (See Genesis 37:23.)

Joseph's brothers did him a favor that day. They stripped off of him what represented his favor in the life he knew, but he would now enter into another phase in his life where favor would not be a label, rather, it would be an identity. That word stripped is an aggressive word. Joseph's brothers didn't saunter on by him and gently ask for his coat. What Joseph's brothers did to him that day gave him the advantage.

Your Holding Pattern

The pit, the prison, and the palace were holding patterns for Joseph's inevitable rise to power. Each stage was a divine incubator for Joseph. The providence of God was laced throughout the entire process of Joseph's experience.

I can remember flying to New York a few years ago. I had to speak at a youth conference in Brooklyn. It was winter, and the weather at the time was inclement. Upon our descent into JFK Airport, the pilot came on the intercom and told us that we were in a holding pattern and could not land until it was lifted. Landing would be difficult because of the snow and ice on the ground, so the pilot flew us around until officials could permit us to land.

At that point, I had a divine moment with God. Many of the delays in our lives are God-designed holding patterns to get us to our destination right on schedule, not too early or too late. Needless to say, I got my message for that night, the holding pattern. All I could do in that airplane was sit there until the hold had been lifted. It taught me how to be patient at the time while people were working out the details on the ground.

Holding patterns are God's safe zones for the believer. It was not comfortable sitting on that plane, yet it was my only choice. My anxiety was not going to make the plane land quicker. The only cure for an anxious soul is to do what St. Peter tells us in 1 Peter 5:7 KJV, *"Casting all your care upon him; for he careth for you."* The Greek word for care means anxiety, and it means to be drawn in different directions. God wants you to cast your cares on Him, not in another direction or on somebody else. You will know his joy once you surrender your concerns into His care.

Just like Joseph, you will have to live through God holding you in strange, even uncomfortable situations. You have not missed your turn; nor has the blessing passed you by. But God is building your character for the palace experience.

It Was Never About You

There will be seasons in the dreamer's life where God will preserve the dream and the dreamer. The dreamer will experience divine protection even in circumstances that contradict the dream. Expect contradiction whenever you are in pursuit of what you have seen in your spirit. It seems as if the pieces will not go together after you see the dream, and this can become very frustrating for any dreamer. You may call this the "doesn't make sense" moment; this is the moment that seems to amplify your struggles while you are working on dream realization. Every great dream attracts great struggle, but the skirmish is only intended to develop the dreamer.

In our lifetime, we have seen dreamers of the twentieth and twenty-first century, and amid conflicting odds, they still dreamed. I mentioned Dr. Martin Luther King earlier in this chapter, yet he remains a notable twentieth-century dreamer. His dream of racial equality and economic empowerment transcended his lifetime, but God used him to blaze a fire that has yielded enormous strides for humanity. What Dr. King dreamed continues to impact generations and cultures around the world; consequently, his dream remains alive even after his death.

Your dream is not just yours to dream, but it is the right of others to do so. Consider the paths that men have trodden to secure a prosperous future, all the calculated attacks on their humanity and integrity, and we can see just how powerful a dream can be. God will secure His intentions in your dream and fuel your efforts so you cannot fail. Let the dream you have seen focus you for the reality you want to live. Having the right focus on your dream will develop an appetite and passion for seeing its fulfillment.

Where is your life headed, and how will you get to that desired place? Your dream will be the guide for you as you navigate through the vortex of change. Circumstances and people will change, but never allow those alterations to change the directive of your dream. The important thing is to allow those changes to serve as life lessons that will establish you for future victories. In essence, change agents become your servants in life. They become the vehicle that moves a generation, a crowd, or a ballpark. Change happens all around us.

Has the melodious sound of the orchestra ever captivated you? Behind the presentation, multiple note changes take the listener through the bliss of that tantalizing musical experience. Who said change had to be devastating? The variations in your life are simply note changes, and if you listen carefully, you will hear the beautiful sound your life was created to make. This is what destiny is, the connectivity of changes, good and bad choices, and strengths and weaknesses that make life beautiful.

The Advantage of Now

Your life represents a series of changes that continue to invite us into more alteration. It is the law of life. Accept that invitation today as you embark on the continuous journey of seeing dream fulfillment.

Faith Gives You the Advantage

Doubt is not the opposite of faith; it is one element of faith.
—Paul Tillich

Isaiah 55:11 (KJV) says, *"So shall my word be that goeth forth out of my mouth: it shall not return unto me void, but it shall accomplish that which I please, and it shall prosper in the thing whereto I sent it."*

In the previous chapter, I mentioned the role of faith in the dream realization process. I want to discuss further on faith and the role it plays in our lives. The child of God must now understand that faith is the only option on the earth today. Faith is the link to purpose fulfillment. It is the legal currency of heaven that can activate God's will on the earth. It is either faith or facts. But what do you do when the facts are hard to ignore, and you have exhausted your resources? Sadly, the average Christian will spend more time believing the facts and not Gods Word. That, however, is not the law of the Spirit. In the world of Spirit, faith is the rule. The Believers act of faith is their response to God. Faith does not cause a positive response from God, but it is your response to what He has already provided. In essence, faith does not move God, faith moves you in position to receive from God.

Faith is the power that takes what is concealed in the Spirit realm and makes it a reality. Because God dwells in eternity and all that God has done is completed from that reality, the believer's faith on the earth gives eternity permission to release what God has already performed. Remember that Kairos time is the time outside of the natural order, Chronos. So, it is not enough to move in time and not have a rhythm with the Spirit of God. Only faith makes that possible. Faith energizes the children of God to march at the rhythm of God's direction.

In the world of the Spirit, hearing always precedes seeing. Faith comes by hearing and hearing by the Word of God (See Romans 10:17.) Faith is activated in the believer by the Word of God when it is heard. So then your faith level is increased or decreased by what you hear. I am not referring to your natural ears but rather your spirit man. The Spirit of God does not communicate to the natural man; rather He communicates to the spirit in man. Revelation 2:7 (KJV) says, *"He that hath an ear to hear, let him hear what the Spirit says to the church."*

In other words, you must hear before you see. The manifestation of what you have heard should be gripped by faith first before it is released by Spirit later. Do not allow what you see with your natural eyes to talk you out of what you have heard from God. This is the challenge for every believer. But if you can grasp this revelation, you will begin to believe to see rather than see to believe.

In 1 Kings 18:41 (KJV), Elijah said to King Ahab, *"Get thee up, eat and drink; for there is a sound of abundance of rain."* It was only a chapter ago, 1 Kings 17:1, that Elijah prophesied that there would not be dew or rain for three years. The Samaritans had been in a severe famine. Food was scarce, and the people were barely surviving. Elijah heard a sound of rain before he saw any evidence of rain. He saw drought, but in his spirit, he heard abundance. He saw barrenness, but his spirit heard, plenty. This same concept applies to the realms of the Spirit, to hear before you see. Abundance is on the way, but if you are sight-oriented, you can miss the supply.

You must believe in your heart what God has shown you no matter the opposition that stares you in the face. The sound was not a natural sound, but it came from the Spirit realm. God was communicating His next move on the earth from the Spirit realm, and that was what Elijah heard. Based on what Elijah heard, his next move would be paramount to the manifestation. As you make decisions based upon what God has shown you, you will find that, as you move in faith, fear opposes your belief. Do not give fear the authority to talk you out of what you have heard from God. Like Elijah set your head between your knees and listen for the rain.

For there to be manifestation, Elijah had to change his location. Often, we try to receive on the level that we heard, but hearing the sound requires that we elevate ourselves. What Elijah heard in his spirit put him in the posture of expectation in the natural. If you hear success coming, then plan according to what you hear. Failed efforts may surround you, but that does not disqualify you from what you heard. Never live on the level of the request, but live on the level of your expectation. If you heard prosperity, then align yourself according to that sound. If you heard healing, then go up to the level where you can see the manifestation. Consider with me that, even though Elijah heard rain but did not see it, this did not at all mean that the rain wasn't coming. Elijah's sensitivity to the Spirit only put him in position to see what he already heard. Faith in God's Word and His promises puts us in position to see the manifestation of His will for our lives.

Once on Mount Carmel, Elijah had his assistant look for a sign. His assistant came back from the first try and said, *"There is nothing."* (See 1 Kings 18:43). The lack of evidence did not discourage Elijah, but at his word, the assistant went back seven times. The seventh time was the jackpot! You can easily get discouraged when sight is not justified by your faith. That's why faith comes by hearing so that, even when you don't see the evidence, you can still hang onto what God has revealed to your spirit. If you have not seen the manifestation of the rain, then the key is not to leave the mountain of your expectation to the valley of discouragement. Rather, it is to keep listening.

A key point I would like to note is that faith is never common sense, it is the power of God. We often look for things to make sense, not realizing that what you are believing God for can only come through the power of faith. Things will not always make sense. When you walk in faith, you walk outside of your senses into the supernatural power of faith. It is the credential that causes you to live in a natural world while operating supernaturally. Faith—and only faith alone—can do that.

Exercise Your Faith

Faith is meant to be stretched like an elastic band, but unlike an elastic band, faith cannot tear if stretched well beyond its limits. There are no limits or boundaries to faith, so faith is meant to be stretched. If you can believe on a thing, you can have it. One area for strength to come is through exercise. You have to work on your faith, give it an assignment, or, better yet, exercise your faith. The exercise of your faith is when you put God's word to the test.

The Word of God is the foundation by which faith stands. The purpose of God's Word is twofold: to accomplish His purposes in us and to bring us into a mature relationship with Christ. It matters what God—not man—says about you. His Word always supersedes the facts and opinions of other people. According to Isaiah 55:9, God's thoughts are not our thoughts, and He always thinks highly about His children. Your faith should stand on what God said because His Word is a sure foundation. It does not matter how people view you. Your faith in God's Word assures you that, if you acknowledge Him in all your ways, He will direct your path. (See Proverbs 3:6.)

People think about you with limited information, and when they are not spiritually minded, their thoughts are limited to the earthly mind-set. God's thoughts about you remain constant even though He knows you will fall short from time to time. God is not trapped in the failures of your present, but He directs you out of your failures into your victory through the victory Jesus achieved on the cross. God's thought about you and I do not change. It cannot. It is so important to embrace God's thoughts of you and reject others' negative opinions as well as the negative opinion you harbor for yourself. In doing so, you will live with the peace of God in your heart.

Prepare to Prosper

You are a result of the spoken Word of God, and God has an obligation to His Word. God cannot lie, and he is therefore subject to His Word. Psalm 119:89 (KJV) says, "Forever, O Lord, thy word is settled in heaven." God speaks, and what He says comes to pass every time. His Word pierces through any resistance you have in your life and buds a new existence within you.

Numbers 23:19 (KJV) says, *"God is not a man, that he should lie; neither the son of man that he should repent; hath he said, and shall he not do it? Or hath he spoken, and shall he not make it good?"*

God's Word comes to prosper you and bring you into boundless joy and peace. It is His promise to you that you should see the fulfillment of His Word. The word "prosper" in Isaiah 55:11 is a verb, and it comes from the Hebrew word *tsalach* which means to push forward. Another meaning is to advance, promote or prosper. However, the root meaning of that word is "to push forward." Because this word is a verb and a verb denotes action, the context is clear that it is Gods spoken word that will accomplish its original intent. The word of God concerning you cannot return empty but must put you in your completed place.

God wants to prosper you and push you forward; this is what prospering does for the believer. It pushes the believer into the place of favor and power. No one can advance or promote you as God can. Let God push you forward into new opportunities that await you. The grace that is on you has already equipped you to succeed on every level you venture into. Embrace it, and let His power flow through you.

Faith Activates the Word

Just like a key is used to open doors and boarding passes permit us to board an airplane, faith also gives us consent to live according to God's Word. We have to believe the Word first, and the Word will carry out its assignment. In Matthew chapter 8, we see a centurion whose servant was sick with palsy, and he wanted his servant healed.

The Advantage of Now

However, because of his position as captain in the Roman army, he felt unworthy for Jesus to come to his house. The centurion says to Jesus that he is not worthy for him to come under his roof, so he asks Jesus to speak the Word only.

Jesus marvels at this man's request so much that He refers to this man's faith as "great faith." The centurion's faith was so powerful that Jesus did not even have to speak the Word. Notice what Jesus says, *"Go thy way; and as thou hast believed, so be it done unto thee."* (See Matthew 8:13 KJV). And before the centurion got home, his servant was healed. The scripture says in Matthew 8:13 KJV, *"and his servant was healed in the selfsame hour."*

I believe God is telling someone, "Go thy way; and as thou hast believed, so be it unto you." If you can believe it, it is already done. So be it unto you. Your body is healed, so be it unto you, your marriage is restored. You will have provision for your vision, so be it unto you. You will prosper, so be it unto you. That job is yours. So be it unto you! God is waiting for you to harness the power of faith with unfeigned confidence in His ability to perform your requests. When you do this, you will see the miraculous take place in your life.

Active Living

God is concerned about our living. He is so concerned that He wants us to "present our bodies as a living sacrifice, holy and acceptable, unto him." (See Romans 2:1.) That word "present" is an active word in the above-noted scripture. It is not the passive yielding of oneself to God that the Apostle Paul is referring to, but it is the active engagement of the human will to God. Not only is the Spirit of God engaging the human will, but the human will must also submit to God. Only a conscious presentation of oneself and a willing attitude can do this. God then is concerned about our current existence, the living we do today. How have I involved God in my life today? Have I consulted with Him about the way I feel? Have I spoken to Him about the weak areas of my life? Faith is most potent when the child of God assumes the posture of a living sacrifice. What is a living sacrifice? It is an attitude of a good conscience toward God. My mother-in-law says it this way, *"A living sacrifice is less of me and more of God in me."*

How are you living? Many times the rush of unexpected trouble can blindside us, resulting in us losing focus on God's Word. Instead of having an active faith, uncertainty and fear cripple our faith. We all suffer a lack of faith in our lives. The person you see who may be walking in the blessings of the Lord was the same individual who had no faith at all at one time. Sometimes it takes us to be faithless, so we can become faith-full. You cannot believe God passively and expect to get results. God wants you to have an active faith, that is, faith that responds to promises of God in your life. To live a life that is active in its pursuit of destiny, active listening is required. If you continue to listen to the opinions of others, your vision will never become a reality.

Anchored by Faith

Jesus will always bring peace to any unstable environment or chaotic storm in your life. While the disciples were on a ship and Jesus was asleep in the boat, a storm arose. This squall was so ferocious that it filled the boat with water, yet Jesus was asleep in the hinder part of the ship. Some would ask, "Why was Jesus sleeping? Doesn't He care about our current condition?" Of course He does, but the message here is that storms are a part of life, and great comfort should be in the fact that Jesus is in the tempest with us. The Prince of Peace was in the ship with them, and He would not let anything happen to them. As children of God, we have to learn to rest in the storms that blow through our lives from time to time. Jesus rebuked the wind and said unto the sea, *"Peace, be still"* (Mark 4:39).

Therefore situations we face in our lives are personalized testing grounds so God can teach us to grow in faith. After all, this is a spiritual journey, and faith is the invisible anchor that keeps us connected to God when life brings different storms. Look at your life today and all the storms you have come through, and you may wonder to yourself,

"How did I make it?" Or someone close to you may look at you in total amazement and question how you have held on for so long.

You may wonder at times, "How did I make it through that storm?" The answer to this question is, "Your anchor keeps holding." The size of the ship does not determine its success. The Titanic was a massive work of creativity and genius; however, it sunk after hitting a massive iceberg on the frigid waters of the Atlantic.

No one sees the anchor that holds the ship in place. They just see that the ship is holding, even in inclement weather. You are that example of that ship that continues to emerge unbeaten and successful even though you have had a barrage of negative circumstances in your life.

> James 1:6 (KJV) says, *"But let him ask in faith, nothing wavering. For he that waverth is like a wave of the sea driven with the wind and tossed."*

Trials and challenges are not the places to waver in your walk with God, simply because what you believe God for requires you to be steady so you can receive what He is giving. The word "wavering" in James 1:6 refers to indecision and instability in the mind. To the natural eye, you should not be making it because of all you have gone through, but what people do not see is what you are anchored to.

You have been tossed with waves of uncertainty, criticisms, rejections, embarrassments, and financial lows, yet you are still anchored to your God. Faith will hold you in place until the storm passes, and you will wake up to the dawning of a new day, realizing that all the storm did was water your faith. So prepare yourself for the most prosperous season of your life. If you are standing in water, all it means is that your seeds are about to bring forth.

The Promise Guides the Process

I promise you! When I get paid, I will pay you back. I promise you! I will be there for the family reunion. How many times have you heard a promise that was not fulfilled? Countless politicians have stood before us and made promises they just could not keep, as well as people in our lives. Sadly, many of those promises go unfulfilled. It takes honesty and sincerity to communicate the intention to carry out those promises, sadly, broken promises at its core is the product of a flawed character. God is perfect, and just in all things; therefore, His word is always sure towards the believer.

Even when we wait on the Lord, God still wants your attention. How many of us have missed trains, planes, or appointments because we were not listening? God requires our attention when we are in wait mode. The primary meaning of the word "wait" is to bind together by twisting.

I have three beautiful girls, and I have the pleasure from time to time of watching my wife do their hair. Apart from the occasional sighs of frustration from my wife and frequent objections from my girls, it is a sight to watch! It is not an easy task because the girls have copious amounts of hair. I would observe my wife braid their hair twist by twist until it was almost impossible for my daughters to unravel.

I believe this is what God wants; to become so twisted up in Him that, no matter how much tension we may feel in life, we will not become unraveled. No matter how negative the situation is, we will remain grounded. Get twisted up in the things of God while you are waiting with an attitude of expectation. Waiting is more than just a process. It is an attitude.

You can get so twisted up in the things of God that you will overcome Satan and his devices. It also stresses the straining of the mind in a certain direction with an expectant attitude. Waiting is a definite part of the process, so the question is, "Am I waiting with a positive attitude to the things of God?" The Apostle Paul says in Galatians 5:1 (KJV), *"Stand fast therefore in the liberty where Christ has made us free, and be not entangled again with the yoke of bondage."*

Satan desires to keep you entangled in everything else except God's will for our lives. As long as you are entangled in the negative, you have no room for the positive. This type of entanglement reminds me of a spider's web. Indeed a spider's web is beautiful to look at when you are not caught in it! As beautiful as that web is, it is a deceptive tool for prey.

Satan wants you to get us caught in his web of confusion, doubt, lust, hate, unforgiveness, guilt, and condemnation, and the list goes on. His whole purpose for doing this is to delay you so we will not see the fulfillment of God's plans for your life. The thing to keep in mind is that God is not miscalculated or misinformed about His plans for your lives. At this very moment, God knows where you are in your heart. Take courage in the fact that God knows. He is omniscient (all-knowing), and His plan will prevail in your life.

Your focus is the key to intentional preparation. When your focus is right, it is almost a guarantee that you will get what you have fixed your mind on. One of the privileges we have in prayer is the guarantee that, when we ask for anything in the name of the Lord, it will be done. John 14:14 (KJV) says, *"If you ask any thing in my name, I will do it."* The key focus in prayer is focus on Him, not on your problems.

This is prayer in its rawest form. It is the fixation of man's heart on God. The name of Jesus gives us access to what is rightfully yours in your prayer life. Put the name of Jesus on that desire to see your body healed, to receive a new house, or to see your family restored or your vision fulfilled. You will see that God will do anything that the name of Jesus is attached to.

Guided by Promise

The children of Israel were guided by a promise through the wilderness despite intermittent turmoil and disobedience. God promised the forefathers of the children of Israel a vast land, the land of Canaan, that was to be divided among the descendants of the twelve sons of Jacob. Upon hearing the cry of the children of Israel, the scripture says that God remembered His covenant with Abraham, Isaac, and Jacob. God had respect for them.

The children of Israel were indirectly affected by a promise made by God to three men who carry massive spiritual influence in the scriptures: Abraham, Isaac, and Jacob. You can be blessed just because of who you are connected to because of a promise that God made to that individual. God made a promise to Abraham that his seed would be blessed, and that blessing applies to us today.

> Galatians 3:14 (NIV) says, *"He redeemed us in order that the blessing given to Abraham might come to the Gentiles through Christ Jesus, so that by faith we might receive the promise of the Spirit."*

In Genesis chapter 15, God takes Abraham for a stroll and asks Abraham to try to number the stars. What an impossible feat! I am sure Abraham looked helpless as he tried to ponder this difficulty when God says to him, *"So shall thy seed be."* And the scripture says that Abraham believed God, and He counted it to him for righteousness. Consider this with me. All Abraham wanted was a son, and it seems like he is tired and frustrated while waiting on God.

Genesis 15:1–3 says,

> *"After these things the word of the Lord came unto Abram in a vision, saying, Fear not, Abram: I am thy shield, and thy exceeding great reward. And Abram said, Lord God, what wilt thou give me, seeing I go childless, and the steward of my house is this Eliezer of Damascus. And Abram said, Behold, to me thou hast given no seed: and, lo, one born in my house is mine heir."*

There is a sense of frustration and restlessness on Abram's part in this text that seems so intense. Has God ever come to you in a vision and told you who He was? Has He ever come to you with a bunch of "I am" statements? And you did not disagree or even refute His claim,

The Advantage of Now

but you went straight to the point as Abram did. "Lord, what will thou give me?"

I know who you are and what you can do, but I need something now. I need assurance now. I need to know that you are here with me now. Abram wanted to know something, just like many of us need God to inject some reassurance in our lives from time to time.

When God said, *"so shall thy seed be,"* it was already done in the mind of God, however, time would just be a passageway for the fulfillment of God's Word. Time does have a purpose, to serve God's commands. Time serves God. On the other hand, time does not serve us, but we are given it as a resource from God to make the best of our lives. Therefore, it is so important that you learn to use your time wisely on the earth, which includes knowing where and how to invest your time. Stop wasting time on things and people you know are not worth your time because time wasted is time lost. Appreciate the value of time by not focusing on what you have lost, rather, on what you lies ahead.

If you are guided by faith and have come into some tough times, do not lose heart. God is just using that time to test His Word over your life. Your faith gives you the power to believe, but obedience is the acting out of that belief. You need an obedient faith in this season, one that responds to God's voice and not your own. Sometimes you have to let the promise that God made to you be a guide in the midst of insurmountable odds. Situations will come to destabilize your faith in the promise, and that's when you must turn to His Word for strength and reassurance. God will perform what He has spoken, and you can take that to the bank.

Will you wait until the sun is shining and the birds are chirping to start that mentoring program or business? Or will we do it when life is against is against us? I am learning that faith does not require my situation to be perfect, but faith can function through the harshest of circumstances. Having faith is possessing the foresight to look past the current situation into the realm of God's promises for your life. Let your faith guide you today.

Giant Advantages

Giants are not what we think they are. The same qualities that appear to give them strength are often the sources of great weakness.

—Malcolm Gladwell

The quote you just read is from the book, David, and Goliath: Underdogs, Misfits, and the Art of Battling Giants. The story of David and Goliath teaches us a lesson on facing our giants and impossible situations. For me, David's story was intriguing, and for some reason, I felt like I was a part of his life. That may sound absurd to some; however, I believe we all see a bit of ourselves in the scriptures. You may not be a David, but you may be a Joshua or a Ruth, and the list goes on. In the life of David, we see God expose the intimate parts of his life. God fillets him like a fish and shows us the heart of this unique biblical character.

There are many advantages presented in the life of David, and I want to take some time and explore the uniqueness of David's life and inevitable ascension to the throne. Just like our lives, God predetermined David's life. Every stage was God-ordained. David was able to take advantage of his time because of the events that would happen in his life. At times, all we can do is sit back and continue to flow in our lives until the right moment.

The Advantage of Now

Once we understand this, it will ease some of the frustration of trying to put things in place and not seeing any results. Know that everything in life is already in place, and it is for us to know when the time is right.

The scripture says in Acts 13:36 (KJV) says, *"For David, after he had served his own generation by the will of God, fell on sleep, was laid unto his fathers, and saw corruption."* David served his generation, understanding God's purpose in his life. Despite David's obvious flaws, God would use him to be an effective leader. The challenge for you and I today is to face the obstacles and opportunities that God has for you in your time. After all, we are born into the circumstances we are born into, to walk with God and bless our generation with our gifts and talents. Many men and women throughout history have made enormous impacts during their lifetime. Nelson Mandela, John F. Kennedy, Abraham Lincoln, and Barack Obama were tailor-made for their time. They could not be born out of that time because they would not have made the impact we read about and are experiencing today.

You cannot saunter on by destiny as if the call of God has not engaged you. The acknowledgment you have a purpose in life requires your full participation. You were created to solve a problem. The goal in life is not to apotheosize the history of your past life, rather it is to make new history. The next day on the calendar should be another page for the history books. Therefore, you must be the initiator of the change you want to see in your life.

First Samuel 16:1 (KJV) says, *"And the Lord said unto Samuel, how long will you mourn for Saul, seeing I have rejected him from reigning over Israel? Fill thine horn with oil, and go, I will send thee to Jesse the Bethlehemite: for I have provided me a king among his sons."*

At this point in David's life, we see God rejecting King Saul from being king over Israel because he disobeyed the commandments of the Lord. God told Saul to smite the Amalekites and destroy them utterly, leaving nothing standing. Instead of Saul following through completely, he kept the king of the Amalekites, Agag, alive and spared all the good things, which included sheep, oxen, lambs, and fatlings.

The Amalekites were known for their brutality toward the Israelites, and this brutality would continue for hundreds of years because of Saul's disobedience. Because of this, Saul lost everything.

Partial obedience will unleash negative circumstances in your lives, especially when God gave you specific instructions to destroy a thing. There is no such thing as partial obedience when it comes to God. And like King Saul, we can end up broken and disconnected from God when we disobey His instructions. What you do not kill early will strengthen itself and seek to take you out later. King Saul had the opportunity of securing hundreds of years of peace and prosperity for future generations, but his disobedience ensured a path of generational struggle. The agony with such a dilemma is that we do not have time to obey God partially. This time requires that you obey Him fully or pay the price for being negligent to His instructions. You may not pay the price in your lifetime, but your household can be victimized by what you do not kill today.

"I have found myself a king." What a loud proclamation from God.

First Samuel 16:1 introduces David in the Old Testament writings. His emergence on the scene is of divine origin. He emerges as a solution to the problem in Israel where Saul was an issue. Saul was chosen king initially because the people did not want to be a theocratic nation, but they wanted to be like the other nations who had men to rule over them. God's plan for Israel was not to be ruled by man. Instead, God intended to rule His people without an earthly king. But the people desired to be like the other nations. They were not content, and they saw their uniqueness as a handicap rather than a privilege from God. Oftentimes you can miss what God has for you because your focus is on becoming something other than what God planned for us. It takes you to be authentic in your originality for your gift to be useful. The world has seen its share of copycats. Your story and your experiences validate your authenticity. You do not need someone else's story. You have your own.

It is impossible for you to miss your time when God is directing

The Advantage of Now

you. Such is the case with David. After Samuel's first encounter with one of Jesse's son's, Eliab, God had to instruct him not to look on the countenance because God does not see countenance. Rather he sees what is in the heart. (See 1 Samuel 16:7.) You see, appearance can be deceiving. The actual measure of our humanity is what lies in our heart, not what we put on our skin. You can dress it up with fine apparel and expensive jewelry, but the heart, not external presentation, gets God's attention. Your heart is the place that God is most intimate. He knows the good and the bad, the strengths and weaknesses. He knows if you are real or genuine.

God was teaching Samuel to discern at heart—not flesh—level. Therein you will find purpose and truth. One by one, God refused all of Jesse's boys. At this point, Samuel must be thinking, "I know I didn't come all this way for God to reject everyone that has passed before me."

After some inquiry, Samuel found out that one son was tending to sheep. David was not in line with his brothers, but he was in line to be anointed the next king of Israel. Lodged somewhere in the Mediterranean mountains under the sun with a shepherd's staff in his hand, he was not with the ones considered, yet God had already considered him from the beginning of time. You may not be in line, but you are next in line to live out God's purpose for your life.

From a Shepherd to a King: The In-Between

David was anointed to be king between the age of 10-15 years old, but he was sent back to the fields to feed the sheep. I like to say that he was anointed for his future but sent back to finish his process. When David was anointed to be king, he was not immediately catapulted into that position, but it would take years until he ascended to the throne. During this time, we see what lay in David's potential reservoir. Apart from being a fugitive on the run from Saul and the chaos that surrounded that time in his life, we see the multidimensional aspect of David's existence.

Ramon O. Gordon

First Samuel 17:33¬–35 (KJV) says,

> "And Saul said to David, Thou art not able to go against this Philistine to fight with him: for thou art but a youth, and he a man of war from his youth. And David said unto Saul, Thy servant kept his father's sheep, and there came a lion, and a bear, and took a lamb out of the flock: And I went out after him, and smote him, and delivered it out of his mouth: and when he arose against me, I caught him by his beard, and smote him, and slew him."

In between his anointing to be king and his appointing, we see bear and lion killers in David and ultimately giant killer. If David were only occupied with what he was going to become, he would have missed those key discoveries that prepared him for his appointment as king. The key here is, while you are waiting on your appointing, be sure to discover all that God has placed within you. The greatest discovery of our true selves is when we are in the waiting process. Downtime is discovery time. Pay close attention to your in-between seasons. Those discoveries cultivate you into wholeness.

Sadly, many of us miss the opportunity to see the multiplicity of gifting and potential that we possess because we are too busy focused on what we have been anointed to become, which can produce an unhealthy anxiety that can leave us unfulfilled. God gives you the process for this purpose, to reveal what else is on the inside of your spirit. You will go through seasons in your life where you will be in kill mode- this is the period between anointing and appointing where you will be forced to stave off certain forces that come to disrupt your ascension to destiny. Kill toxic relationships and character defects that can threaten your pursuit of destiny.

Yes, you are anointed to be king, but while you are in the process, embrace those moments that reveal the bear, lion, and giant killer in you. I do not believe that David was sitting around waiting to be king, but he was busy in the process. The same process that had him occupied revealed his other strength's gifts and abilities.

There is a multidimensional person in you that's waiting to show itself. The process will reveal what is in the package, but if anxiety is pushing you through your process place, you will miss the key transitional points that reveal the greater picture of your destiny.

David's story is germane to many of our life experiences where we must live through the process until fulfillment. The purpose of David's process was to develop him to rule Judah and Israel. Just like him, we are in the process from shepherd boy to king. Making shepherd boy mistakes at kingship levels should be avoidable. So the process is a vital step to gaining wisdom and maturity for the journey. Therefore, discipline is an essential aspect of growth. It is easy to recover at Shepherd level than king level because each of those arenas carries various levels of accountability. Each level contains a level of publicity and prominence.

In biblical days, being a shepherd was an important job, but it was not glamorous. Shepherds lived apart from society and were nomadic based on job description. Coincidently shepherds were the younger sons of farming peasants who inherited no land. Remember, the firstborn received the inheritance, but David was the youngest.

Mistakes made at shepherd level may be what I call "progress blunders." These may not be fatal in the beginning but will be lethal in later years if not dealt with swiftly. In between the anointing and the appointing, you will have progress blunders, the mistakes that occur as we grow into our purpose. Some of the development blunders include but are certainly not limited to mismanagement of funds, bad decision-making habits, and poor judgment, and the list goes on. When we continue to commit detrimental blunders without checking them with sharp rebukes and active reconstruction, we fuel a ticking time bomb of self-destruction.

Inquire

The first thing that David did was ask about the rewards for killing the giant. His motivation was clear; his size or inexperience did not deter him, but the incentives motivated him. King Saul promised three things to the man who would kill this giant: great riches, the king's daughter, and the freedom of his father's house from debt.

David saw the opportunity and seized the moment. Not only would David's victory guarantee his gain, but his triumph would also remove the burden from his household. When you decide to fight your Goliath, you will not just personally benefit from it, but it will also profit those around you. He did not let what he heard motivate him temporarily, but rather let what he heard motivate him enough to follow through with what he felt in his heart. David experienced his Kairos moment, his time to take advantage of the situation.

Be motivated by what you hear and not what you see. Sometimes the driving force behind what we do must be the outcome from what we heard. To hear something and not seize the moment will guarantee defeat, but to hear and do, will ensure victory. I am not sure how many men thought about fighting Goliath, but David did not think too long before he acted. David understood the advantage that he had because he had God with him.

Maybe the incentives for slaying certain giants in our lives are having a healthy marriage or peace of mind. However you look at it, you reap the benefits from slaying the giants that stand in the way of your progress. Israel was in a stalemate with the Philistines, and nothing pointed toward progression. But as soon as Goliath was slain, they were now in a better position to advance their kingdom.

What is standing in the way of your progress? What is blocking the view of your vision? When you identify what obstructs your progress, you can now choose the tools you will need to position you for victory. It is not the size of the opposition in front of you that is the threat; it is the size of your perspective that can easily talk you out of your victory. Some of the perspectives you nurture in your mind are products of your upbringing. Maybe certain family members had certain biases that have shaped their philosophy, and if you allow those views to become your own, you will always remain small in your mind. You see,

God wants to blow Himself up in you so that all you see is victory. To see your way forward, you must move your Goliath.

First Samuel 17:33 (KJV) says, *"And Saul said to David, thou art not able to go against this Philistine to fight with him: for thou art but a youth, and he a man of war from youth."* Goliath's résumé speaks for itself when we see him matched up against David. No one knows how old David was when he fought Goliath, but many scholars note he might have been between fifteen to seventeen years old. He could not be twenty years old because all his brothers were twenty and over, the requirement to be enlisted in the army in those days; his age was not the factor at this point.

Israel needed a hero, and a shepherd boy would be the one to deliver that victory. Faith and confidence are the tools that guarantee graduation in life. You have to be willing to step up to the challenge when everyone else is frozen in fear. David's courage put him in position for promotion. Courage will always put you in a position of action while fear will keep you frozen in inaction.

Take Off Saul's Armor

When you were born, you were equipped with everything you needed to live a victorious life. No one is born with a shield, gun, or a knife, but with time, you will see a steady progression of growth as you submit yourself to the process of learning. As you grow, you adapt to your environments, and ultimately learn what your strong and weak points are.

Even in David's life, you will notice that he succeeded at different stages of life because God was with him. Saul places his armor on David and sends him out; however, it was weighty, and David did not fight with Saul's armor before. (See 1 Samuel 17.) What worked for Saul in battle would not work for David, and you will see that Saul killed his thousands, but David killed his ten thousands. You see that Saul's armor was competent to his level of potential, thus his thousands. Would David have killed his ten thousands if he had on Saul's armor? I seriously doubt it.

For David to be successful in battle, he had to take off the provisions of Saul and rely on God's formula for success. You can become dependent on a man, but that can become a hazard to your potential victory. David could have been armor-dependent, and history could have been read differently today. Our generation needs more people who will be courageous enough to face the goliaths in our modern day culture. David tried on the armor King Saul provided, only to take it off because he had not proven it in battle.

The Challenge

Do not look at Goliath as a challenge but as an opportunity for God to use you to conquer your enemy on a major platform. Of course, Goliath was a giant warrior in Philistine who had terrorized the land for decades until he met David. Every David has a giant; every giant has a David. The common thread between the two is time. Goliath was a threat to Israel for a long time until a young shepherd boy ran toward the challenge. David ran towards Goliath with speed and maneuverability unburdened by armor.

You must be willing to run toward the giants in your everyday life with a mindset of victory. People who know who they are will not retreat into obscurity, but they will use the challenge as a platform to solidify their victory. I believe that this is what God wants from all of us, to see the opportunity in our giants and not the intimidation.

When we see this perspective, it will make it easier to have the right mindset to win. Maybe the giants in our time, such as poverty, abortion, teen pregnancies, and terrorism, have not met the giant in you. David, by all standards, was much smaller than his enemy was, but his heart was big. And while Goliath was much larger than David was, God was with David, which placed David in a great position. Put on your spiritual goggles and see miniature David going up against a massive Goliath. In the natural, Goliath looks like he will obliterate

David, but in the spirit, David has all the host of heaven backing his every move.

Choose a Stone

> First Samuel 17:40 (NIV) says, *"Then he took his staff in his hand, chose five smooth stones from the stream, put them in the pouch of his shepherd's bag and, with his sling in his hand, approached the Philistine."*

David chose five smooth stones from the brook but only used one. One of the things that the Holy Spirit taught me when I was teaching this message was, "You have many options, but you only have one choice." David chose five stones but only used one. Sometimes we put all our eggs in a basket because of the enormity of a struggle or the size of a giant in our lives, or simply our anxiety can trigger certain actions that can affect our lives.

You will need a strategy to defeat the giants that lurk around, intimidating you causing you to retreat and stick your head back into your shells like turtles. I call this the turtle complex. When you peep through the opening to see if the threat is gone, to your dismay it is still present. The turtle complex may protect for a while, but it does not eliminate the threat. Unfortunately, that thing, that giant, that persistent problem, is still there waiting for your response. The giant you are facing in your life will go down, but you need a strategy to secure your victory and ultimately your future.

David prepared for battle by choosing those stones. No sword, no shield, no armor. What you choose will work for you. Have confidence in this truth. If you trust God with your challenge, you will see victory in every area of your life. Choose with the intent to win the first time. A way to assess your challenge is by setting out your goals and carefully putting them in proper perspective. David did not waste time trying to convince himself that Saul's armor might just work. If it's not for you, it is not for you. Here are three things to consider while you are assessing your goals:

1. Figure out what the goals are. Be honest with your assessment, and move on your instinct in dealing with your challenge, whether it may be a challenge with building your credit, raising your children, or difficulty on your job. Be honest about your current position.
2. Determine if these options can meet your goal. It is an unfair expectation to think you have to fit a certain criterion in order to face your challenge. Remove yourself from that burden.
3. Face it. No task or goal that you will not confront will remain a threat to your destiny. So, to overcome, you must confront. Regardless of what the challenge may be, facing it is the key. Leap into the challenge with unwavering focus.

David's immediate absence when all of Jesse's sons, except him, were presented did not mean that David was not on God's mind. David was already on God's mind, and his absence only validated his authenticity. I believe that isolation is the place that is closest to God. Sometimes this is where God must set us so we can see ourselves and, most importantly, Him. Divine experiences happen when we are by ourselves. Moses met God on the backside of the mountain. Ravens fed Elijah by the brook Cherith, and the devil tested Jesus after a forty-day fast. John was on the isle of Patmos, and he saw great revelation. I will deal more extensively with isolation in chapter eight.

What you can hear and see are amplified in your lonely times because you are now able to see and hear God. God has consumed your heart with His presence and infected you with His love. Isolation is the place where God primes you for the place that is prepared for you. You are not off track. God is using that isolative state to form a winning character in you. The Bible says that David ran toward Goliath. What intimidated everyone else about Goliath did not bother David, but he ran toward that giant with fearlessness and determination with the will to win. The posture every successful-thinking person must adopt is one of courage and determination in the face of impossible odds. The Bible says that David ran toward the giant, and while he was in pursuit, he reached for a stone. Not only was David in the posture of pursuit, but he was also composed enough to gather his weapon. Now is not the time in our lives to fumble, when we are going in for the kill. If David dropped that stone, history would have been recorded differently. Have you ever been at a place in your life where this was it? You lost battle after battle, and now you have a chance at redemption. The obstacle in front of you may be significant, but its size should not decide your competence. Determination, focus, accuracy, and execution were the forces behind David's swing. I want to coin the term the "DFPA swing," literally the power behind the swing.

- Determination is the ability to focus on your giant's destruction in the face of opposing forces and those who do not believe you are competent. It is your inner drive to succeed in spite of what you face. See that giant fall before it hits the ground!
- Focus is seeing through your inadequacies first and identifying the weakness in that giant in your life. Often the weakness in the opposition is the strength you need to carry out the attack. Focusing on what limits you will limit you.
- Accuracy is the result of determination and focus because they help to line up the target. Your ability to be accurate is the result of your calculations and adjustments that were made before the pursuit.
- Execution is where you deliver the final blow with force. This power comes from knowing you have made the necessary steps to achieve your victory. Your execution is the moment the stone leaves your sling and the instant your giant hits the ground.

Please understand that whatever you are pursuing in life, whether it is a college degree, a stronger marriage, overcoming poverty, or

Ramon O. Gordon

addictions, you cannot do any of these things with unnecessary weight. Take the active role in shaking off whatever is holding you back, and with all the energy you can muster, hurl that stone toward Goliath's head!

What's in Your Hand?

What seems insignificant to the world is a tool used by the hand of God to impact the world.
—Ramon O. Gordon

Leadership has been one of the most studied subjects on the planet. Seminars, symposiums, and conferences cater to leaders and leadership styles of all sorts. Although attending seminars, discussions, and conferences are beneficial for continued learning, they do not force leadership out of the individual. It takes learning from our experiences today and reaching back for the nuggets from past experiences that cultivates the leader within us. I am learning that leadership has to be developed through the classroom of time and experience. You see, only experience can teach what college universities and seminaries cannot. Those mediums are powerful tools to gain the principles, but the privilege of experience is that you can exercise those principles in real-time situations.

I try not to take my building moments for granted but use them as platforms to harness the lessons I have learned. Most times the pain of the experiences secures the foundation upon which you will build your success. As a young minister, I have observed the ministries of influential pastors. I have profound respect for any proponent of the gospel, and I have even tried to emulate some, but I have found out that they were products of their own experiences, as I would be a product of mine. Another pastor's life experiences cannot be lived out through my life, but I can use his experiences as a reference for my path. Your experiences teach you how to be authentic; they teach you how to appreciate your originality. Most of us find ourselves after we have tried to be like everybody else.

The emergence of the leader within you will meet the demand of the chaos outside of you. For the leader to emerge out of you, it must also go through the chaos within, to meet the demands in your world. You are the answer to a problem, but the leadership consciousness must now emerge. The world is not short of problems; therefore, leaders are always in demand. What are your guiding philosophies? Consider with me that the wrong philosophy can sabotage your life. At the core of our existence are guiding philosophies that influence our decision-making. Get the right philosophy. Doing this means we have to discard our memory bank of the conditioning of old thought patterns.

Where will you be when that moment comes? Moses met his Kairos moment when he met God at the burning bush, a moment that would change his existence and ultimately the lives of millions of people. As you continue to live, you will find out that God has strategically carved out moments in your life that are designed to reveal His purposes in your life. When you come into the knowledge of your identity, it will change your life forever. Moses was a fugitive on the run from the Egyptians, but he was a captive of God's divine providence.

To those of us who do not think that God is concerned about what we go through, well, He is! God is so concerned that He will come against powers and authorities to see about His children. God saw the affliction of His people, and He wanted to bring them up out of the land of Egypt into a land flowing with abundance. (See Exodus 3:17). God wanted to bring the children of Israel into their flow. The text describes it as a land flowing with milk and honey. Notice the key word, "flowing." The Amplified Version describes it as a land that is good and large, a land of plenty. The land that was promised would be a place where provision and favor were continually flowing; the word flow means to move in unbroken continuity, uninterrupted, and uninhibited.

God has designed a flow for you, a place that is tailor-made to meet all your unique needs and even wants. God wants to get you to your flow, a place where we could enjoy the rewards of His grace. He desires to bless you and bring you into long-lasting prosperity. God heard the cry of His people, and He appointed Moses to be the leader who would carry this burden.

The initial issue with the children of Israel was not that they were not a mighty people, but their mentality was steeped in servitude and not ownership. The Egyptians took advantage of this opportunity and exploited Israel's ignorance. If not careful, your ignorance can become somebody else's advantage.

When you do not know who you are, you will let people exploit you and keep you in a place that's convenient for them. Nobody except God should ever have that power over you, and God brings His perfect will into your life, regardless of how it may look or feel.

Exodus 1:7–10 says,

> "And the children of Israel were fruitful, and increased abundantly, and multiplied, and waxed exceeding mighty; and the land was filled with them. Now there arose a new king in Egypt that knew not Joseph. And he said unto his people, behold, the people of the children of Israel are more and mightier than we: Come on, let us deal wisely with them; lest they multiply, and it come to pass, that, when there falleth out any war, they join also unto our enemies, and fight against us, and so get them up out of the land."

The king of Egypt set taskmasters over the children of Israel to keep them in bondage, they afflicted the children of Israel and made them serve with rigor. But the Bible does let us know that the more they were afflicted, the more they multiplied and grew. This situation seems odd to me. It would seem to me that they would get weaker with every abuse they suffered under the grueling Egyptian sun. This proves there is a purpose in affliction.

Two things happen whenever you are in affliction: you multiply, and you grow. The Apostle Peter tells us in 1 Peter 4:12 (KJV), *"Beloved, think it not strange concerning the fiery trial which is to try you, as though some strange thing happened unto you."* In the backdrop of this text, fire spread though Rome, and the Believers were blamed for the devastation. Consequentially, the Believers were targeted by Nero, murdered in savagery fashion, and lynched. The fiery trials that we experience throughout our spiritual journey are a part of God's design in molding and making us into the image of Christ. It is not strange; it is purposeful, and they are to be expected. The many sufferings we endure are according to the will of God, and His will is always perfect.

Imagine the struggle to want to be free, but because of fear and insecurities, the Children of Israel choose to stay in bondage. Sometimes the fear of not knowing what lies ahead of you can keep you in bondage to a system or routine. But you must break free so that you can make the trek towards destiny.

Even amid extraordinary affliction and hardship, God was still with the children of Israel. And God is with you in your Egyptian experiences. As they cried, we call out in anticipation of God's help. The children of Israel cried, they cried out to God for deliverance, and God heard them and had respect for them.

The times were hostile in Egypt, but God had a plan during it all. He always has a plan when times seem difficult and full of adversity. The environment in Egypt was aggressive, hardship and turmoil had gripped the Israelites and they were desperate to be free. It would surely take a leader with the power of God to be used as a tool of deliverance. In this instance, God's plan was in Pharaoh's palace in an adopted son by the name of Moses. The purpose for Moses being born was to be a vessel by which God could use to deliver His people.

Notice that God had to partner with man to achieve a goal. It has been this way from the beginning, man partners with God so God's purpose could be accomplished on the earth. Man is only the vessel, but God is ultimately the force by which purpose and intent exist. You do not have to die in your hardship because God has ordained a Kairos moment for your advantage. God heard the affliction and cries of His people, and this sets in motion what God had already predetermined in eternity.

From a leadership standpoint, Moses stands tall in mind. God gave Moses certain qualities that are still relevant to leaders today. Leadership qualities were already in Moses as he was raised as a prince in the Egyptian palace. With the pre-leadership role and when the times demanded of Moses, those qualities came to light. The task to deliver the children of Israel out of bondage was an enormous responsibility; however, God destined for him to fulfill this task, regardless of his inexperience in active leadership.

I would like to make the point that leadership can be birthed out of inexperience and even failure. Not all failures are created equal. There is a context associated with that failure that can help to avoid fatal repeats. Mistakes will be made on the route to destiny; it is an integral part of our humanity. Bill Gates started a company called Traf-O-Data, and it failed miserably. He dropped out of Harvard, but his passion and vision reassured him another opportunity as he launched Microsoft. And we see history being made every day.

The truth is that, when you are destined to win, nothing can stop you from reaching your goals and dreams. Nothing! The key to achieving victory over failure is not to stop the progression of your vision, but to learn from the lessons from failed places and continue moving forward without any reservations. Your failures will put you in the flow of uninterrupted success, and you will be able to bless another generation through your experiences.

Purpose in Isolation

It is critical to note that Moses led his father-in-law's sheep through the backside of the desert, and in this isolated place, he met God. You cannot escape God's presence. There is no place that is so remote and restricted that God cannot get to, whether it is a geographical location or your heart, God has access anytime. King David said, *"If I go up to the heavens you are there, if I make my bed in the depths, you are there."* See Psalm 139:8 (KJV). God met Moses in a place far from human interaction, a location of dryness and total quietness. There was no noise, just Moses, and God.

Moses was isolated, but God was with him every step of the way. God orchestrated the palace and the desert experience; it was always a part of God's plan. Maybe Moses was frustrated because it seemed like his life came to a sudden halt after running as a fugitive, but not in God's mind. Even on the run Moses could not escape God, because it was God's plan the whole time. How many desert experiences have you had that you tried to run away from, not knowing it was a meeting place of the divine? It is a place of equipping and preparation, not a location to run from. It's a place to embrace God's will for your life.

Often, solitude is the best place to reboot our minds and ultimately our lives. It is here that God's Spirit ministers to us in times of need. After Jesus overcame the temptation of Satan, angels came and ministered to Him (See Matthew 4:1-11). There is also a therapeutic element to loneliness where we can see ourselves and find ways to deal with new personal discoveries. Princeton's word net says that isolation is a state of separation among persons or groups or a feeling of being disliked and alone. I believe this definition holds true to many of us seeking out a better way with God. Sometimes we are isolated because we are too unique to blend in with anything or anybody else.

Your assignment on the earth can be the force that isolates you and stores you for divine use. Quick note: low self-esteem will make someone relate to something less than who they are when proper focus should be given to their vision. If the vision that God has given you is bigger than you are, that is what you should be looking toward, because you cannot become what you will not focus on. Set your affection on things above, or fix your focus on what is above you because you will become what you behold.

Types of Isolation

Consequential isolation is a result of negative behavior patterns from an individual. When certain negative behavior patterns go unchecked, character can become embedded in error. There are consequences for everything we do, whether positive or negative. Therefore, it behooves us to walk sensitive to the operation of the Holy Spirit in our lives.

Another type of isolation is divine isolation, where the individual is set apart by God for specific use. An example of divine isolation is when the Apostle Paul writes in Galatians 1:15 KJV, *"But when it pleased God who separated me from my mother's womb, and called me by his grace."* Normal becomes a foreign word to you when you are set apart. While everybody else is meeting at the local diner, you are on your knees in your prayer closet. While folks are engrossed in the television, you're moving in the vision God gave you.

Divine isolation is the last stop before God catapults you into the world with an anointing to tear down Satan's kingdom. Matthew 4:1 (NKJV) says, *"Then Jesus was led up by the Spirit into the wilderness to be tempted by the devil."* Jesus would fast for forty days and nights as God prepared Him for His earthly ministry. After this experience, Jesus's life and ministry would never be the same again. Signs and wonders would flow out and through Him, giving light to the works of God on the earth.

Next is familial isolation. When God has called you, many times family will be the first group of people to misunderstand the calling. Because of the call of God on your life, they will rebuff you. People reject what they do not understand. Similarly, People tend to form opinions of themselves that are below their expectations. Then those same people get upset when you decide to break the mold to live your best life. This, my friends, is not your burden to bear. Psalm 27:10 (KJV) says, *"When my mother and my father forsake, then the Lord will take me up."*

Family forsakenness is common when you begin to move in the things of God. If you have the audacity to believe that you will live the abundant life while the people in your family are content living in poverty or ignorance, then get ready for isolation! Your audacity to believe threatens the people around you. Never let the low self-appraisal of others define how you see yourself. Dare to see yourself above and not beneath, lender and not borrower, head and not the tail. Never abandon your passion for God to stay where others are comfortable with you. Break the mold!

What Is in Your Hand?

Many times we feel unprepared because we focus on what we do not have and neglect what we do possess. However, it is what you have that you have taken belittled that will bring you victory in your life. Never downplay the little bit that God has given you because little can become much if it used correctly. Shepherds used two types of tools in biblical days: the rod and the staff. The rod was about a yard-long stick with a knob on one end.

The staff, also known as a shepherd's crook, looked like a modern cane. The rod was used to guide the flock in and out of pasture, and it was also utilized to protect the sheep from danger. Other uses include disciplining the sheep if they ventured too far from the herd. Every now and then, the shepherd would have to lead the flock through treacherous terrain to find pasture, and the shepherd needed that rod to guide the sheep effectively.

The tool that Moses had in isolation became the one that God would empower him to use to show signs and wonders in Egypt. Moses had a rod he had used for forty years, tending the flock of Jethro, his father-in-law, in Midian. God would use this same tool to do exploits in Egypt. Moses did not have to go looking for another tool, but God supernaturally empowered what was natural. Can you imagine what was going through Moses's mind? Some would say a staff is nothing more than a glorified stick! What sort of extraordinary miracles can this staff produce? However, the common will become great through God's anointing.

What is in your hand? Could it be the thing you have carried for years that God is going to use? Maybe it is your talents, abilities, influences, or your resources, such things should never be seen as menial or insignificant. To Moses, the rod was a natural tool, but God saw it as a spiritual resource. All God had to do was put His supernatural on Moses's rod and there would be signs and wonders. Whenever you release your natural, God's supernatural will take over, and you will live a life of total victory.

It is unhealthy to look on someone else's work ethic and envy their success. Commitment and resilience are the two engines that fuels a successful person's rise. You must commit to the goal and you must find strength to bounce back when things don't go as planned. Do not envy others. Check your arsenal of tools and you may find that you possess the right tools that will give you the cutting-edge approach to the success that you envision. To say you do not have enough or your tools do not work correctly is to say that God gave you something that was defective. This notion is incorrect because God cannot give out something that has defects. He can only give out something that is perfect. Most times it isn't the tools that are dull, but it is our perspective that needs sharpening. Sharpen your perspectives and your tools will deliver every time.

James 1:17 (KJV) says, *"Every good and perfect gift is from above, and comes down from the father of lights, with whom there is no variableness, neither shadow of turning."* That scripture speaks about the act of giving. What God has given you and I originates from something we cannot see with our natural eye. There is nothing wrong with the gift; however, the prevailing issue is the character of the one that has been given the gift. You can be gifted to run a Fortune 500 company, but a flawed character will rob you of the integrity needed to safeguard the power and influence of your name.

It is critical to note that good leadership is not just highlighted when pastures are green, and the ground is fertile, but good leadership should be equally emphasized when the ground is dry and the land is barren, yet there is production. Effective leadership is the ability to lead out of something that is barren into something that is fertile or produces. This was the job of the shepherd. His job was to navigate through rugged terrain and uncertain circumstances and find a place where the sheep could get nourishment for their bodies.

This is what leaders do. Leaders navigate. They find places of pasture and rest for the ones they lead. Moses led the sheep on the backside of the mountain, searching for a place for them but ended up finding himself in the presence of the Almighty God. Please consider with me that Moses was a leader, but even leaders need time with Lord, moments of refreshing and anointing. Never dismiss your isolated or lonely seasons because it is that place where God seeks to develop you and awaken your consciousness to the gifts you already possess. Lonely seasons are designed to get a yes out of you, to solidify your "Yes, Lord!"

"I Am" Sent You

God will prepare you for what He has called you to because His name is on your assignment. God has given you an assignment. You cannot go in your name. You must go in the name of the Lord. Moses inquired of the Lord what he should say when he got to Egypt, and God instructed him to assert, *"I am that I am hath sent me."* Moses realized his human limitations and knew he needed God to back his every move to carry out the assignment.

My brothers and sisters, God's backing is always guaranteed. His name is on your assignment, so get failure out of your mind and replace it with victory. If the "I Am" sent you, you will fulfill your assignment. The word in Hebrew for "I am" is ha-yah. It means to be, or I am. God says to Moses, "I do not have a beginning or an ending. I did not come from anywhere; I am not going anywhere. I am consistent with My eternalness, and will never change, I am." Anywhere God sends you, the power of the "I Am" is present with you. Failure is impossible when the "I Am" God is with you. When you are assured that God's presence is with you, then you will possess the confidence to carry out the role for which you have been chosen to do. The issue is not if you are competent enough, but it is the fact that your confidence must rest in God's ever-abiding presence.

Moses is not the only scriptural figure whom God sent, but there is a plethora of other men and women whom God sent to do His will. You are privileged to join this remarkable list of men and women who did something for God. And just as they were relevant to their time, you are relevant to this time. That means your gifts, talents, abilities, and even struggles all play a role in the empowering of today's generation.

Reaching for your gifts and talents will further put you in position to change lives through you. The truth is that we should leave the earth a better place when we leave it and not add to the calamity. To do this, we cannot be like the world, decked out in its cultural perspectives and trending thoughts, but we should have a mind like Jesus Christ.

Mission-Minded

You must have a mindset for the mission if you are going to be effective at carrying it out. What is your mission statement? It does not have to be long but must be concise, so that when you read it, it lights the flame of urgency in you to get some things done.

Mission-minded people:

- Seek out the harvest of the world. The world is rich with trends and cultures, yet it is waiting for the culture of the kingdom in you to invade the cultures of this world.
- Have different worldviews. Their thinking is not denominational, organizational, but it is purely about Jesus Christ. They are flexible and adaptable. Most importantly, they are not easily offended.
- Mission-minded people hear and obey the voice of God and share the love of God anywhere they feel the leading of the Spirit.
- Make disciples. Jesus says in Matthew 28:19, to *make disciples*, which means that we teach and show the love of God to new

converts so that they can infect somebody else with the love of God.
- Go into all the world!! No matter where that is if it is a place, we are commanded by Jesus to go.

A victorious mindset must precede the victory; it empowers you to continue believing in yourself because God can only do it through you. Rid yourself of the religious theology that God is going to do it. God has already done it! In time, however, God is looking to do it through someone. God is seeking to work through your intellect, creativity, ideas, and, ultimately, life. Your mind holds your ideas, intellect, creativity, and plans.

When you submit yourself to God, He will work through the above-stated capacities. He is only limited when you live by fear and low self-esteem. Often your frustrations indicate that not enough of your ideas are being released out of your mental space. Have you ever asked yourself why you were frustrated? Your mental space does not have a limit in what it takes in; however, without executing your ideas, you can live a difficult life, never actually flowing in the expression of your victorious self because of doubt and fear.

Leadership Identity

Real leadership is not contingent on somebody's age; Wisdom is simply a by-product of experiences. It is achieved through those life lessons that the leader goes through that prepares him or her for leadership roles. In many ways, those experiences give you the advantage as you enter into leadership roles. Preparation indicates leadership consciousness- this is where the leader will prepare for what is to come, whether he or she is in leadership roles.

Sheldon Stryker wrote a journal on "Identity Theory and Personality Theory: Mutual Relevance," in which he theorizes that the concept of identity salience is elaborated from the multifaceted view of self. He goes on to say that self is conceptualized as comprised

The Advantage of Now

of a set of discrete characters, with persons having potentially as many identities as there are organized systems of role relationships in which they participate. He embellishes the fact that we are products of our environment and products of the roles played out in our lives.

In this study, people were used as social objects in positional locations in society assigned by others, and they were observed to see how they would conform to their environment. After some time each test subject would conform to their environment, which reduced their ability to stay authentic and true to their identity. The leader within you will not allow itself to become compromised by the environment around you. As negative as the circumstance can be, leadership must emerge.

The scripture says in Colossians 3:3 NIV, *"For you died, and your life is now hidden with Christ in God."* When you gave your life to Christ, you found a new identity. No longer do you have to associate with the identity of your past life, because you are new in Him. The more time we as individuals spend trying to be somebody else, the less time we have to be who God has designed us to be, so get busy at doing you.

Your ideas, intellect, creativity, and plans are enough to get the job done for you. Therefore, it starts with how you view yourself, not how others perceive you. When you begin to collaborate with the right people, you will strengthen the perspectives needed to make sound destiny decisions. The leader in you is currently in student mode as you learn how to grow in grace and character.

Placement and Promise

There was no lack in Eden, and if Adam abided in the will of God, everything was always ready for him.
—Ramon O. Gordon

In the beginning, God! Those four words captivate the minds of thinkers everywhere, especially in theological circles. The question is asked, "Does God have a beginning?" And the answer remains, "God has no beginning." Moses said in his prayer to God in Psalm 90:2 (AMP), *"Before the mountains were born, or before You had given birth to the earth and the world, even from everlasting to everlasting, you are [the eternal] God."*

God is unchangeable, and He is eternal. Therefore, eternity is not ruled by time as we are. God is outside of time, yet He is involved with human beings in the realm of time. Genesis 1:14 (AMP) says, *"Then God said, "Let there be light-bearers (sun, moon, stars) in the expanse of the heavens to separate the day from the night, and let them be useful for signs (tokens) [of God's provident care], and for marking seasons, days, and years."*

The words "seasons" in this text means appointed time; it also denotes change. In chapter one, I deal with the Greek thought for time. However, I want to elaborate more on time regarding seasons. King Solomon wrote in his book of wisdom, *"To everything, there is*

The Advantage of Now

a season and a time to every purpose under the heaven" (Ecclesiastes 3:1 KJV).

We live our lives in seasons, and in those seasons, God has appointed key destiny events to take place. You must be sensitive to the season if you are going to receive what God has appointed for you. Ruth was in the right place and met Boaz. (See Ruth 2.) Elisha was in the right place when he got a double portion from Elijah. (See 2 Kings 2:9.) The 120 in the upper room were in the right place when the promise of the Spirit came to the earth. (See Acts 1:15.)

Whether your movements are circumstantial, the moves you make define the season you are in. God gave you seasons as an agent of time that carries you to your destined place. Each new season in your life brings meaningful change. Change surrounds us all; it is a constant that will remain for the rest of your life. Each passing season in your life, whether spiritual, physical, or emotional, brings you closer to the purpose God has ordained for you.

The Bible says that the sons of Issachar understood the times (See 1 Chronicles 12:32). Although the Sons of Issachar were skilled warriors, they also understood the times. They knew what was happening around them and could realign themselves, and the nation of Israel according to that knowledge. They could discern what God was doing and when He was doing it. Their understanding of the times made them relevant, not outdated. They had an incredible advantage! No one, no system could keep the Sons of Issachar out of the sphere of influence in Israel. The nation of Israel followed them and waited for their guidance. Like them, we all should strive to understand the times we live. In that, we will find our next proactive move in the earth. Proactive movement requires discerning to know the times in which God currently has you.

At times, in your discernment, you will find God telling you to remain in a place for a time until His purpose has been executed. The Bible says in Acts 1:4 (KJV) says, *"And, being assembled together with them, commanded them that they should not depart from Jerusalem, but wait for the promise of the Father, which, saith he, ye have heard of me."* I referenced Acts 1:15 earlier in this chapter, and I want to point out some key points. Jesus tells His disciples in Acts 1 to not leave Jerusalem, but to wait for the promise of the Father. Notice, the place and the promise were connected. The promise of His Spirit would be released in Jerusalem and nowhere else; therefore, this is where they had to remain. There will be waiting seasons in your life that cannot be dismissed. If you are going to have that level of power that only the Holy Spirit can produce, you must remain in the place God has instructed.

Once you understand that your destiny requires that you must follow a path, you will know the importance of placement. There are no detours or alternative routes to destiny. Whether you believe it or not, the place you are now in is a tool in the hand of God for you to understand that God is the ultimate strategist who created an environment for man to live in and thrive. The place that God has designed for you is of vital importance to your process. In many ways, it can be a holding pattern for you as He cultivates your character for your destiny. Although circumstances may indicate otherwise, you are on track to collide with your destiny.

Empty Voids

The Bible says in Genesis 1:2 (NKJV), "The earth was without form, and void; and darkness was on the face of the deep. And the Spirit of God was hovering over the face of the waters." Those two words, "form" and "void," are important in understanding a deeper spiritual significance. The word "form" in the Hebrew is to-hoo, and it means desolate or to lie waste. And the Hebrew word for "void" is bo-hoo, and it means empty or nothingness.

The earth was desolate, lying waste, and void, then the Spirit of God moved. Then God spoke, and what lied bleak, wasting away, and void took shape and form after God said, "Let there be." Often, we find ourselves at various stages in our lives, as the earth was, formless and void.

We are like empty cisterns with the inability to keep substance, and consequently, we are wasting away, but God's Spirit always fills a void. God wants to fill all your voids with His presence. Voids left because of absentee fathers, negligence, or abuse is ready for the love of God to consume that space. It is not uncommon to go looking for ways to fill a void when you are hurting. I have seen where people seek to escape their pain through drug use, only to find their reality still intact after their euphoric experience has depleted. The temporary relieve is just a band-aid, but God wants to heal you from your pain. You may leave the external place of the pain, but the internal pain will still go with you. Leave a city, change jobs, and in some cases, some people change their names, but internally you are wired with safety checks to detect a repeat of past events. Until you are healed, you will leak out of your core self, leaving you present in the world but lacking the zest and thrill for life. God's Spirit comes to heal you and if you receive the goodness of God in your life, your days will be satisfied.

The Perfect Environment

The Garden of Eden represented an ideal, a spiritual principle. Eden was the perfect creation with fresh vegetation and breathtaking scenery. It was the garden of innocence, where man could walk before God naked and ashamed. Eden was the picture of innocence. It was the place of eternal fellowship with God. It was also the site where disobedience broke the symphony between God and man. Eden was where man embraced his supernatural abilities and used it to glorify God. God's original concept of man is in Eden. The man who is full of God's breath, the one who is God's likeness and image, will live out his purpose.

God communed with Adam every day. Because Adam could not ascend to where God is, God had to come to where Adam was. This is what is called anthropomorphism; the term comes from two Greek words: Anthropos (man) and morphe (form). Therefore, anthropomorphism is when God appears to His people, manifests himself in human form, or even attributes human characteristics to

Himself. When God made Adam, He made him from the dust of the ground. The body was man's container until God breathed into man. Nothing was hindering God from communing with man's spirit. God did not visit the animals or take a stroll down Eden Boulevard to see the exotic plants. Rather God visited the spirit of man. He spoke with Adam openly and intimately. There was no lack of revelation. Whatever Adam wanted to know, God told him. For a while, we lost that connection, but it has been restored through our last Adam, Jesus Christ.

Find your Automatic

When you find your place in the earth, you find your automatic flow.
—Ramon O. Gordon

The blueprint for living and the expectation for mankind is laced in the book of Genesis. God planned to have somebody reflect Him on the earth. So much so that, when that man was looked upon, he would know this man reflects God. He is not God, but he reveals God. You and I are the reflection of God on the earth. I want to state that it is God's plan for you to live out the meaning of your existence on the earth. You have been placed here for a purpose, to come into a relationship with God, assume responsibility for your gifts, and live out His purposes.

Genesis 2:15 (KJV) says, *"And the Lord took the man, and put him in the garden of Eden to dress it and keep."* God put Adam in position and gave him his first job, to dress and keep the garden. Man was always meant to work, but God intended for man to enjoy his work. Notice, Adam did not have to go looking for a place or a job, both were provided. That was God's responsibility. When you walk in sync with the heart of God, He will supply you with the position, description, and resources for your life. This was not strenuous work or hard labor. All Adam had to do was think the perfect environment, and his thoughts would produce.

God is not the kind of creator that abandons what He creates, but He assumes responsibility for what He creates. God is not like man. He does not flee under pressure; He takes responsibility. When you find your place in the earth, you find your automatic flow. The garden of Eden had to produce whatever Adam wanted because Adam was in constant connection with God. It was a Spirit to spirit relationship that nourished Adam in the garden. God's relationship with Adam formed an environment of spiritual utopia. Find your automatic. There is a place programmed to give you whatever you ask. It is a place ordained by God. Man was already in place. He did not have to go looking for another place because he was at home with God.

As long as Adam was in Eden, he was in the place of eternal provision and purpose. Parents are only bound to take care of their children until they leave the house and most cases that does not happen. However, the Garden of Eden housed all of Adam's needs and wants. He did not have to go looking for anything outside of Eden, but Adam disobeyed God's instructions, and the ramifications would be catastrophic. Disobedience to God's commandments shifts you out of the eternalness of God into the order of time; which is a demotion. It stops the flow of spiritually induced progress and makes you reliant on Chronos time.

There was no lack in Eden; all Adam had to do was stay in Eden, and everything was always ready for him. If you are in the will of God, you are in your Eden. Do not allow disobedience to escort you outside the realms of supernatural provisions. As I stated earlier, the garden of Eden was not just a place, but it represented an ideal. We are not at the place, but we can bring the concept with us. Health, wealth, and prosperity are all concepts of God's original plan for man. He wants His children to be healthy, wealthy, and prosperous in all areas of life.

The garden of Eden can be in your marriage, career, or life. Imagine living in a state of constant provision with no lack. Imagine having a life where you never run out of anything! Remember, God's original idea was that we would be in a continual state of supernatural living and abundance, not lack and anxiety. God wants this for His people, to live in His provisions. Jesus Christ has made this possible for us. After Adam sinned in the garden, humanity was subjected to a sin nature. (See Psalms 51:5). And not just that, we were born with a sinful nature and were objects of God's wrath. The only way to redeem man and give man back his dominion was for a perfect, sinless man, Jesus Christ, to die. Christ died in our place as our substitute. Adam was a representative for humanity, but Jesus Christ acted as our representative on the cross to redeem humanity from their sin.

Control Your Space

It is critical to point out to you that you have inherited dominion from God because Jesus recaptured that authority through His sacrifice at Calvary. You have been given authority in this earthly realm to be as creative and intentional as your Heavenly Father. To rule, reign, and have dominion is in our spiritual DNA as human beings. Embedded in the core of our spiritual selves is that absolute law, to have dominion. That word "dominion" means authority, rule, or realm. So God has given you authority to have dominion in the earth realm. God has put you in place not to be controlled by the place, but to live out the purpose of God in that very location. Poverty, racism, unemployment, and disease do not define your place in the earth, because God has given you dominion to live above the negative facets of our society. Now is the time to use your governmental authority as children of God to live out your inherent rights as Kingdom believers in the earth realm.

  A person's environment is significant to their overall success or failure, what surrounds you can either have a positive or negative influence on your behavior. One way to foster a healthy environment is to practice the art of avoidance. This task can be difficult and requires discipline and instincts to execute efficiently. Avoidance does not mean absence. It means putting into practice a set of disciplines that help to keep you focused on your destiny markers. Nonetheless, when you are purpose-minded and purpose-driven, you will do what needs to be done, to see your goals realized.

An Original

The word "created" in Genesis 1:27 is Hebrew in its origin. It is bara (pronounced "baw-raw"). Bara means, to create or make. This verb is of profound theological significance since it has only God as its subject. Only God can create in the sense implied by bara. The verb expresses creation out of nothing.

The scriptures use the word "formed" in Genesis 2:7. It is an English word and Hebrew in its origin. The word is yatsar in Hebrew, and it means to form, mold, and fashion. When God formed Adam, he molded him into a desired shape. Adam was perfect according to God's standard, not men's. If there were an imperfection—and I am sure there was from a human standpoint—he was still perfect in God's eyes. Adam's height, weight, and hair were perfect. He lacked nothing. Like Adam, you have been formed by the Creator. He planned your life before you were born. You had a purpose before you took your first breath. Our creator molded us into a desired shape, and he expects us to move on the earth according to His design. God wants His children to be what He has designed them to be not a replica of somebody else's life.

God wants you to live according to His design, not your desire to be like anyone else. God was the first architect, and male and female were His first design. Remember, the word "created" in the text means to create out of nothing. There were no supplies, only a thought. A design is simply a plan. Except this plan was in God's mind before it was released on the earth. Please understand with me that a thought is just as powerful as the real thing; however, it takes faith to pull that thought out of the womb of your mind into existence. An architect exercises his or her plan through contractors. They have to explain what they want and set a high standard. But God exercises and executes His plan through His Word and His Word only.

God took time designing each one of us. We are all fearfully and wonderfully made. We are made according to His standard, and not others'. This is where we should place your confidence, in the fact that God has made and fashioned you according to His liking. Stop looking in the mirror trying to determine what is right or wrong with you, and look to God's Word as the ultimate tool of reflection. If you see yourself through God's Word, you will see what is truly wrong. If you see yourself through others' opinions, you believe a lie and not the truth of God's Word.

All God had to do was speak His Word, and whatever He spoke came into existence. God said, *"Let there be light and there was."* God said, *"Let there be lights in the firmament of the heaven to divide the day from the night and let them be for signs, and for seasons, and or days, and years."* And it was so.

So whatever God attached His Word to came into existence. God attached His Word to you, and you came into existence, and He is not through with you! God would never have attached His Word to you if He knew that He would not get anything in return. In other words, God invested His Word in you, and you will see the results of His Word manifest in your life. In Genesis chapter one, God spoke to potential, and potential had to yield results. Even now, God is speaking to your potential self, the best in you wrestling to be released this very moment. Only this time there will be no struggle because Gods word is activated in your life. The Spirit of God is moving you from your potential self to your actual self this very moment, and your life will never be the same again!

Out of a Thought

Change your thoughts and you change your world.
—Norman Vincent Peale

Norman Vincent Peale, the father of positive thinking, quipped, "Change your thoughts and you will change your world." This is not a possibility, but it is a reality that belongs to those who are willing to change the way they think. Our thoughts make up most of who we are as individuals. They connect us to our inner selves. Having control of our thoughts gives us the advantage when we set out to implement change in our lives. Everything begins with a thought.

Our thoughts are like the incubators that protect newborn children. Inside the incubator is an environment that is conducive to the continued development of the baby. But that environment is only temporary, and at some point, that newborn has to leave that incubator into the atmosphere of its new world. Like the incubator, our mind houses our thoughts. It is an environment that can be helpful or detrimental to a person's life. The breakthrough you seek in your life is waiting for the development in your thought life.

Ideas are simply thoughts, but those thoughts will remain locked up in the womb of your mind if you do not have a plan. Greatness begins with a thought, but it does not end with just a thought; it must end with action, which will create results. Actions create results, but you must direct your actions toward your dominant thought. In truth, the life that you live can be shaped by dominant thoughts, those same thoughts mold our belief system which in turn decides our actions. Are you loyal to a belief system that does not match your core value presently? You see, as human beings we are ever evolving, so what was important to you then may not be important to you now. Therefore, it is imperative to listen to that dominant thought as it takes you through the journey of life towards a better you. Your thought life is the gateway to the springboard of life. A successful diver always picks a spot before he or she completes a dive. They do not just plunge themselves into the water without being intentional. Your success will not be predicated on whether you made it to the springboard, but is predicated on whether you took the dive. Many have approached the springboard of their dreams, only to bounce around in uncertainty and fear, never launching themselves in the possibilities of success. It can become easy to get complacent in the act of doing something but fail to spring from thought to action. Certain thoughts serve as a springboard that can propel you into your destined place.

Stop wasting time on jobs that do not challenge your potential because that only places your energy in the wrong place. There is nothing worse than placing your energy in a job or task that does not challenge your real potential. Now do not go out and quit your job because you've found this newfound zeal. Zeal will not pay the bills. Some jobs must be endured for a season so you and your family can be taken care of until other doors of opportunity begin to open.

According to an article in the Washington Post written on May 20, 2013, 27 percent of college graduates have a job-related to their major. Millions of dollars of student loans are waiting to get paid back from people who are not even using their degrees. Most settle for survival jobs such as bartender, restaurant hostess, servers, and so forth. This simply means that survival jobs will maintain a certain level of living. Unfortunately, there is a ceiling. Your true purpose is deeper than just a college experience. You would be surprised at the percentage of people who are unfulfilled, yet they have graced some of the most prestigious schools in the world.

As believers, God does not want you just to survive. He wants you to thrive. Placement is critical to surviving because you cannot be productive in a place that is not conducive to your overall mental and spiritual growth. To try to make my point clearer, the cactus is a plant that lives in a habitat that is subject to drought for extended periods, and the environments are extremely arid. Not only does the cactus plant survive there, but it also thrives in these conditions simply because of its unique water conservation abilities. The roots on the cactus spread out to collect water when it rains and stores it for future use. However, you may not be a cactus but a Dahlia plant, which can only survive in wet climates. The key here is knowing where you fit and where you do not fit. You were created to thrive, prosper, and flourish. When the Spirit of God is flowing through your mind, you have the advantage over any situation. Dry climates, wet climates, good times and bad times cannot defeat you because you are directed by the Holy Spirit in you.

When you are purpose-driven, you will live a life of total fulfillment as you operate in the call that God has placed on your life. However, a survivor's mentality will make you choose what is inconvenient for you, which will keep you in bondage. The key to living a purpose-filled life is to live according to God's thoughts of you, which you will find in His word, the Bible.

Jesus Thinking

Jesus thought unrestricted and independent from the religious system in His time so His mind could be available to God. When you think like this, you automatically attract enemies. The Pharisees and the Sadducees were prominent religious sects in Jesus' lifetime and beyond. They were religious in thought and action, yet they lacked the spiritual discernment to flow spontaneously for God, and they were no real threat. The threat to your purpose, however, can be your thinking. Jesus understood this, and He flowed outside of the religious restraints of the system. Throughout Jesus's time on the earth, His mind was always connected to the Father, who was the source of everything that he said and did. Jesus operated outside of the religious expectations of men and lived according to His purpose.

Once you free yourself from the restraints of negative thoughts and expectations from men, you will then avail your mind to God. Some norms are designed to keep your mind limited to the social, political, and religious status of your present world, and this threatens your ability to avail your mind to God.

Why is this so critical? The mind is the key to propelling your life in the direction God purposed your life to go. Like the rotors that steer the boat in the desired direction, so your thoughts steer your life. The world is waiting for your way of thinking, your ideas, and your thoughts because these are what identifies you in the earth. They are the link to your mind. When you think of the Apple software, you think of Steve Jobs. When you think of $e=mc2$, you think of Albert Einstein.

Nothing that has ever made it into the Greatness Hall of Fame is ever anonymous because a name is attached to that success. This is exactly why someone can never take credit for another man's work. You are God's original, and you can never be duplicated.

Hear and Do

Greatness and influence are birthed out of thoughts, imagination, and ideas, and without these, you can be a known as a great thinker but not a doer. Having an imagination is being able to create a visual on the canvas of your mind, and your ideas put that masterpiece into perspective. Your imagination is your creative power and ability. It is the key to turning what is imagined into a reality. Using your imagination requires mastering your visualization.

In other words, never let what you see with your natural eyes determine what you believe God has told you. When other people see a mess, you see potential. By visualizing potential in a mess, you create an opportunity for the masterpiece in the mess to be revealed. Like the stroke of every paintbrush on a blank canvas, you must begin creating the masterpiece of your life. You are in your blank canvas season, a chance to start painting the future you envision. With the stroke of your brush, God can bring meaning to what may seem abstract in your life. Each stroke on the canvas of your life may seem abstract to some. However, it is your visualization that gives you the advantage.

Clothe Your Mind

> Philippians 4:8 (KJV) says, *"Finally, brethren, whatsoever things are true, whatsoever things are honest, whatsoever things are just, whatsoever things are pure, whatsoever things are lovely, whatsoever things are of good report; if there be any virtue, and if there be any praise, think on these things."*

If your mind had a wardrobe, what would it be dressed like? Would it be rags or riches, negatives or positives, good or bad, or peace or chaos? You are what you think. I am sure that you have heard the slogan, "You are what you eat." That is very true. You are what you think is equally as valid. It is time to start thinking right about ourselves. Thinking positively will allow you to embrace God's peace in your life, especially in times of chaos and uncertainty.

To move forward into your destiny, your mind must be in the right frame of thinking. Look at the framework of your mind, and determine the thoughts that make up that framework. Maybe there has to be a flushing out of old thoughts. Thoughts that shaped what and who you were from your past life should not be what guides you in this new season of your life. It is difficult to control the thoughts that enter your mind, however, it is through the Word of God that you are able to discern the thoughts that will help you reach your destiny.

The human brain is powerful. It manages the data that comes into your minds. It is easy to be bombarded daily with subliminal messages, whether through television, or even a conversation with a co-worker. Some things you do not need to hear, so it becomes mandatory that you hit the reset button in your mind. Don't refresh, reset! Because hitting the refresh button is only going to recapture what formerly existed in your thought life. However, when u reset your thoughts, the Holy Spirit blows fresh thoughts into your mind. Our experiences in our lives shape us all. All of us have various life dynamics that contribute to who we are today. Those experiences, whether good or bad, are meaningful and advantageous to those who will see the purpose they serve.

The mind can become a place of clutter if not given a routine cleansing. If you look in your junk email inbox, you would be surprised to see how much junk email you see. To free up your mental space, you have to delete the junk mail in your mind. Reset your mind. Go in and clear out those things or people who only contribute to your junk inbox and not your destiny inbox. We all need a reset from time to time, a chance to step out onto new frontiers of thinking. The blessing in this is that you do not need permission to do this. When you decide to hit that mental button, your life becomes new. Your reset moment is waiting on your decision to engage in the pursuit of your destiny. Never underestimate the power of your mind, it has the power to help you overcome your obstacles so that you become what you envision.

Think Forward

You cannot think the past and at the same time gain the future. Your past may be a conglomerate of good and bad choices, regret, guilt, happy times and sad. But looking forward is always the key to progression. The right thoughts will shape your expectation, so you will not waste time with something or someone who does not fit the framework of the life God has for you. Also, the right thoughts help you to make wise choices and avoid those decisions that can stagnate your progress in life.

Keeping your mind occupied with your mistake or misfortune

will only plunge you deeper into the pain of regret. This mindset is very detrimental because you will now spend your energy living to undo the mistake. But the only thing you can do is move forward. The Apostle Paul admonishes us that we should be renewed in the spirit of our minds.

Ephesians 4:23 (KJV) says, *"And be renewed in the Spirit of your mind."* The word "renewed" in the text does not speak of the mind itself, but it talks about the spirit of the mind, which the indwelling Holy Spirit influences. Renewal is necessary because you can become so stretched in your situations that it makes it difficult to believe the word of God. All of us as believers need to be renewed in our mental space because life can hit us with so many unexpected blows. Sometimes poor choices are results of the unrenewed mind, and we need to be renewed from that old system of thinking that has plagued our lives. Many times, what believers call spiritual warfare are just results from poor decision making. It's not the devil; it's the decision that often demonizes our lives.

The unrenewed mind is the mind that has an appetite for the carnal nature. That word carnal means pertaining to the flesh. It wants nothing to do with God, consequentially opposing the law of God. The Bible says in Romans 8:7 KJV, *"Because the carnal mind is enmity against God: for it is not subject to the law of God, neither indeed can be."* The Apostle Paul says that the carnal mind is enmity against God. The word enmity means hostility. So, the carnal mind is hostile towards God and His word. It rejects fellowship with God and holiness; it is Satan's playing ground. Satan wants to control your thinking through your carnality, which is connected to your five senses. The unrenewed mind is your antagonist. But the Holy Spirit nourishes and influences the renewed mind through your faith. He does not control your will, but He speaks revelation to your spirit man, which in turn helps to combat the hostility of your carnal nature. And when this happens, you cannot resist His influence.

The Bible says in Romans 8:6-7 AMP, *"Now the mind of the flesh* is death [both now and forever—because it pursues sin]; but the mind of the Spirit is life and peace [the spiritual well-being that comes from walking with God—both now and forever]; 7 the mind of the flesh [with its sinful pursuits] is actively hostile to God. It does not submit itself to God's law, since it cannot." You must develop your mind to think according to the spirit and not the flesh. When you think according to the flesh, you think limited, but when I think according to the spirit, I think potential. Not only that, I think as Christ thought in the earth. Spiritually minded individuals produce thoughts that are conducive for growth. It does not mean that an idle thought will never cross your mind because they will. However, the spiritual mind thinks life and peace, which combats the hostile thoughts implanted in your mind through your circumstance. The carnal mind is controlled by your senses which is connected to your world, while the spiritual mind is connected to Jesus Christ through faith. When you understand the supremacy of Christ in your life, then you will realize the power you have over your carnal nature and live a victorious life.

Think the Right Outcome

Will I think faith or fear? Will I think power or weakness? Will I think peace or chaos? Where you are now is not permanent but temporary. You will move toward your future with clarity and determination, but the right mind is needed. Which mind are you connecting to while you navigate through the vicissitudes of life, your carnal or spiritual mind? Your outcome will depend on the dominant mind in your life, for within that mind lies your advantage or disadvantage. Every day is a battle of supremacy for the dominant thought. The world of Spirit and flesh engage in this endless battle until the mind that wins ultimately becomes you. The bible says in Proverbs 23:7 AMP, "*for as he thinks in his heart, so is he.*" The word heart comes from the Hebrew word leb, which refers to the immaterial personality function of an individual. It does not speak about a person's exterior; rather it focuses on what takes place internally. You are not governed by your environment, but you are controlled by the spiritual mind which is controlled by the Holy Spirit.

Your mind houses the vision and the destiny that God has given; however, this cannot become a reality until you exchange my old thoughts or thinking patterns for new thoughts. Your carnal mind nurtures thoughts that are hostile towards your spiritual self. Its goal is to discredit the word of God so that He will no longer control you. This is the tactic that Satan used against Eve in the Garden of Eden. He said to Eve, *"Yea, hath God said, ye shall not eat of every tree of the garden?"* (Genesis 3:1 KJV). His goal has been and always is to keep his thoughts dominant in your mind so that you forget what God has said. When God thoughts take root in your mind, Satan no longer has control over you, because you are connected to the fountain of living water.

The right attitude becomes the catalyst for a productive life. It is the springboard for success. It is hard to get anything done when you do not have the right attitude. Author and motivational speaker, Zig Ziglar, said, *"Your attitude, not your aptitude, will determine your altitude."* You may not be the most gifted or the most qualified, yet the right attitude can propel you into unbelievable success. From time to time, we will encounter trials that will cause us to develop negative attitudes. The Spirit of God must control our perception of the trial if we are going to have a positive outcome. You can be immersed in the most negative of circumstances, and the right attitude can give you the right outlook. Attitude is everything. It is what seasons your day and produces results.

Let His Mind Control You

The mind is the meeting place of all battles, spiritual and carnal. Winning the battle in the mind is paramount here because it is the final frontier of all humanity's struggles. Win the battle in the mind, and you win the battle over the flesh. Frankly, winning this battle will not be easy. It will take submission to God and His word to defeat the constant battle of the flesh. The bible says in Galatians 5:16, *"This I* say then, walk in the Spirit, and ye shall not fulfill the lust of the flesh." That is a guarantee!

The Bible says in Philippians 2:5 (KJV), *"Let this mind be in you, which was also in Christ Jesus."* The scripture you just read is of profound Christological significance. Here the Apostle Paul exhorts to humility, as well as living a life of selflessness. To have the mind of Christ is to think and act the way he did. It was a mind emptied of its self-interests and fixed on the heart of God. This is the key to our advantage in any situation, having the mind of Christ in operation in us, but we know we are being controlled by the influential power of the Holy Spirit.

The Holy Spirit implants thoughts into your mind to help combat the old nature and its depraved way of thinking. Jesus' thought life was powerful, becoming the ultimate model of submission for all time! When you submit your mind to the Divine, the supernatural will automatically flow in your life. There was this urgency to do the will of the Father, and the infusion of the mind of God in Him propelled Him to complete His assignment. Whenever you have the mind of Christ, you cannot escape the process toward destiny fulfillment.

Jesus was in the garden of Gethsemane when he asked the Father to let this cup pass if it were possible, but instead, he surrendered His will and said, *"Nevertheless, not my will but thine be done."* (See Luke 22:42.) Jesus surrendered His mind to the will of God in the middle of His greatest mental fight- this is a pattern that we all should follow as sons and daughters of God, and that is not to choose our will as the path of escape, but His will as the path to destiny.

It is what you think about God that will decide the outcome. Your God concepts are birthed through your circumstances, but they are not controlled by those circumstances. The God concepts will develop the right perspective that will hep you to overcome the challenges life brings. When you raise God up in your mind, you raise your mental capacity to think as Christ thought.

What about the Rest of You?

God Begins where you decide to End.
—Ramon Gordon

Watching movies is one of my favorite pastimes. There is nothing more thrilling to me than watching The Godfather marathon or The Bourne Identity with Matt Damon. You know when a movie is not good when you have to ask the question, "Wait! Is it over?" No climax. No punchline. Nothing tantalizing to leave the viewer in a state of awe.

By no means am I a movie expert, but I have seen enough movies that have compelled me to ask that question, "Is that it?" Perhaps the screenwriters ran out of ideas, or their concepts were too bold and did not complement the ending. As I said, I am no movie expert, but nothing beats a good ending!

I think that many of us had reached a place in our lives when we asked the question, "Wait! Is this it?" The anxiety that goes with pondering that thought can set someone in a dangerous state of mental debilitation, and I view this sort of question as constructive.

It is like the college student who graduates with a degree in biology, only to find out that she has a passion for the arts. What this means for her is not that she wasted four years, but now she has to take inventory of her gifts and incorporate her four years of learning into the discovery of her new passions.

Once you take inventory of what lies in your arsenal of talents, ideas, and abilities, you reach a place where you surmise that, with all you have to work with, is this it? It is a question of consciousness that cannot go unanswered. There is nothing more frustrating than knowing you can do and accomplish more, but you reach a block on the path to discovery. When you know you can do more, do more.

No, where you are in your life is not the final place. There is more that God has planned for you. You must now take the right inventory of your life and make those necessary adjustments, so you can fulfill your destiny. You are on a new horizon in your life, positioned on the brink of new discoveries. God is the ultimate source that you will need as you use your gifts and talents on this new horizon of your life.

Recently, as I was going through years of note taking, I noticed a quote I made, "The right outlook requires no solution for how things will be accomplished, rather the right outlook is rooted in hope." In many ways, how we view ourselves can taint our outlook on life. We want to feel secure in knowing the outcome. We want the solution to the problems before we even embark on the journey of novel self-discoveries. God told Abram in Genesis 13:14 (KJV), *"And the Lord said unto Abram, after that Lot was separated from him, Lift up now thine eyes, and look from the place where thou art northward, southward eastward, and westward."*

Notice that God told Abram to look in all directions. And this is what God is telling you today. Stop limiting the scope of your vision to one direction. Your vision was meant to be multi-directional. You were made to reach outside of the norm of your culture and challenge the status quo. God told Abram, "As far as your eyes can see, I will give it to you." What an incredible assurance. As far as your eyes can see, what you see is yours. Regardless of where you are today. You may be standing in the doldrums of an adverse circumstance yet it is from that place that God wants you to see your vision.

True progress requires three things:

The Advantage of Now

1. The first thing it needs is introspection. Introspection is a looking inward or examining your internal space. The word "introspection" means "observation or examination of one's own mental and emotional state, mental processes, etc.; the act of looking within oneself" (dictionary.com). Its synonyms include contemplation, meditation, reflection, and, worse yet, scrutiny. No one I know enjoys looking at themselves, especially in the negative aspect of their humanity. The problem is within. This practice serves to bring our inner selves to the reality of the truth. We come face-to-face with our greatest antagonists, ourselves! Not our mom, dad, sister, or brother, but ourselves. Introspection is self-inspection without the remedy. A few years ago, I called an exterminator to come out to our home to check for bugs. Spring season has a funny way of introducing new friends! After the inspection, the gentleman told me his recommendations and dropped a bomb on us! Not just a few bugs, but termites! Thankfully we got to it early! This discovery prompted a new strategy and timetable. They would have to bring out the big boys on this one. That introspective moment was when the exterminator examined our home, but after that, he had to call in the specialists who knew how to take care of the problem. You see, God is the only one who can take care of our internal conflicts.

2. Secondly, you need retrospection. Having a healthy outlook requires retrospection, the action of looking back on or reviewing past events in your life. Although this can be painful for many, it can also be helpful in fostering the proper outlook on life. Do this knowing that you cannot change the past, but you can accept the past for what it was, and use it as a springboard for what will be. You cannot enjoy the wide-screen view of the future ahead of you while looking back in the rearview mirror of the past behind you. Isn't it funny that the rearview mirror is smaller than the screen in front of you? That is God saying to you that the narrow perspectives of

your past only serve one purpose, to show you that what you went through prepared you for your future. The Apostle Paul had a retrospective moment when he said, "Forgetting those things which are behind, and reaching forth unto those things which are before, I press toward the mark for the prize of the high calling of God in Christ Jesus." (See Philippians 3:13-14 KJV.) There must be a goal that is attainable for you. Without a goal, you can live presently but stuck mentally. Crime scene investigators go back to the scene of a crime to look for clues that can help an investigation, even long after the offense has been committed. Retrospection is like the scene of a crime; it has clues that will help you avoid repeats in your future.
3. Thirdly, foresight is the act of anticipation or the act of considering what will be; it is an invitation from the future to our present that keeps us alive to see all that God has for us. Webster's defines foresight as "thoughtful regard or provision for the future." Foresight is a strategic implementation of plans geared towards. Project yourself into what the future holds and work yourself backward as you determine the steps that need to be taken to experience that future.

Don't Hide Your Fire

Who can hold fire in his or her hand without it burning at some point? It is impossible. Fire cannot be contained; it can only survive with oxygen. Just ask the brave firefighters in California who tackle the wildfires that ravage through acres of land. It is harder to contain because of the oxygen that is available to feed its unrelenting path of destruction. Let's look at what Jesus says in Matthew 5:15 (KJV), *"Neither do men light a candle, and put it under a bushel, but on a candlestick; and it gives light to all that are in the house."*

To contain that light is to deprive yourself of your pathway and ultimately the path of others. That candle just does not give light to the one holding it, but it provides illumination to the whole house. When you do not burn, someone else cannot see his or her way through life. Unfair? But it's not. We are all connected through life, and we all need someone to help aid us on our journey. Do not look at it as a burden. See it as a privilege to be able to be a light to someone's journey. What is burning in you that is the answer to poverty and hungry children? Or what is calling you to public service or ministry?

These questions need honest answers, and once you find that truth, your light will begin to lead and guide through the process of becoming what God ordained for you to be. Someone is waiting on your light to help them in their pathway. Your communities, your country, and the world is waiting for your light to shine. Once you find your light, shine! That illumination in you is God working as the oxygen that feeds your spirit and builds your capacity to contain Him. He fans the flames of your passions and burns your vision so you cannot stay still. The Prophet Jeremiah said it this way, "I tried to keep quiet, but it was like fire shut in my bones." (See Jeremiah 20:9.)

Escape Normalcy

The cost of escaping normalcy is dismal in comparison to the price one pays when he or she cannot be identified as unique anymore. Life has a way of defining what is normal for you if you let it. Be willing to shake up routines to come into a greater understanding of your purpose. As new worlds open for you in your relationships, businesses, or career, always remember that the old routine won't survive in that world. As you ascend the ladder of change in your life you will be catapulted into new systems that will demand that you adapt, or you can get left behind.

The steps you apply to your life today will help lay the foundation for your new normal. Be not conformed to this world, but be transformed by the renewing of the mind. (See Romans 8:1.) Real transformation is the result of a changed mind, and an altered mind cannot accept a barren season as its normal. I alluded to Sarai and Abram in chapter six, and I would like to address it further. (See Genesis 11:30.)

Sarai was barren. Nothing was producing for her at all. She had no children. Ultimately Abram could not be the success he was supposed to be without Sarai, so God speaks to Abram and says, "Go, leave this land and go to a land I will show you."

Abram could have stayed in Haran because he and his family had been there for some time, but destiny will never let you settle. Just because your things are settled in a place does not mean you are settled in your spirit. Your spirit man is under the influence of the Holy Spirit, and at this very moment, He is searching your heart, and He knows God's intentions for your life. (See Romans 8:27.)

What happens when you find yourself at the crossroads in between comfort and the unknown? You follow your instincts until you find your place. It almost seems unfair for God to give Abram a command to leave his comfort zone for a land that God was going to show him. After all, it is not like God gave Abram a longitude and latitude. God just told him to go!

Many times, we check out God's forecast, looking for the predictable, but God cannot be predicted, He must be taken at His word. I have seen weather forecasters predict rain on Monday, but the sun shined on Monday, and it rained on Tuesday. What am I saying? Weather forecasters predict the weather using models and computers, and they use the knowledge of trends and patterns. However, God's assurance is in His Word. As soon as God says it, it is already guaranteed to come to pass. If He says to look for rain today, expect it. Look at God's pattern in the lives of His people, and you will see His track record.

At times, our limitations help us to discover our differences and in turn use that knowledge as fuel for our lives. Those differences are the commas in our lives that reveals a greater meaning to our lives. What may be viewed as a limitation is simply an advantage in disguise. Hellen Keller became deaf and blind before her second birthday. Despite this debilitating disability, she learned to read and write, and she became the first deaf-blind person to gain a bachelor's degree. She campaigned on issues of social welfare, women's suffrage, and disability rights and impressed many with her resilience and personality. Hellen Keller did not have an opportunity to define her new normal, yet despite her challenges, she did not let what was normal for her keep her down.

Beethoven started going deaf at twenty-six years old and went completely deaf at the age of forty-six, yet he is remembered as one the greatest composers to have ever lived. For a musician to lose his or her hearing is one of the greatest misfortunes ever imagined, but it did not stop Beethoven. Despite the great anger and frustration, he produced classics. Beethoven experienced normalcy for some time before he went deaf but would have to adapt to his changes to redefine himself. He had the benefit of hearing before he went deaf, so after going deaf, he was able to use his memory as a reference for his many successes.

All of us have been dealt unexpected cards in our lives, but those do not define the rest of our lives. They give us the advantage to adapt, cultivate, and build on what others consider as insurmountable odds. The two individuals I mentioned in this section are just a small fraction of the masses of people who have learned to build on their limitations. When building on your limitations keep in mind that weaknesses aren't really weaknesses, but they are undiscovered strengths.

Begin!

God's Word cannot return to Him empty, but it will accomplish or bring His divine purpose to fruition. It is all about beginning. But beginning anything can be a tedious task, especially when you have followed a pattern of failure for a period. Here is the great thing about patterns, they can be broken! Most of the things we enjoy today are results of what began.

Apple's first computer was built in a garage in Cupertino, California, and today the company is a front-runner in innovation and creativity. Amazon.com is the world's largest online retailer, but it began in Jeff Bezos's small garage in Seattle. The garage served as an incubation period until the vision these men had gained traction through their tireless work.

The Bible says this about beginnings, *"Do not despise these small beginnings"* (Zechariah 4:10 NLT). Do not allow smallness to define where you are going. God has a way of taking a micro thought and making it into a macro life. If you can get discouraged in your building stage, you won't be able to enjoy the building in its completion. When you can conquer your fear to start a business or a church, apply for college, or launch a new app, you position yourself for future successes. Do not allow the perception of failure in your mind to halt you in your steps. Fear should motivate to get things done.

When you are focused on your plans for your life, you become sensitive to new ideas, and you entertain thoughts that will challenge you to begin. Destiny does not begin in the plushness of comfort zones, but it starts in oily car garages or smelly mangers with farm animals, as our Lord began. Stop trying to soften your response to your vision by justifying your level of comfort. It will not manifest until steps are taken to begin what God has placed in your spirit to do. Sometimes it takes being in uncomfortable situations to bring about fresh ideas and cultivate imaginations.

Please know that, as you live, the plans, people, and places will begin to unfold for you. God has ordained it so that everything you will need to push your vision forward is already in position. The place, the people, and the funding are strategically in place by God until the appointed time. God has chosen you to share your vision, and He has chosen and set aside people to help you accomplish that vision. Everything needed for your vision to thrive is already in place. You now must get in place so the synergy among your vision, the people, and the place can blend into a masterpiece of God's providence.

Think according to the vision God has given you and not according to the circumstance that you are in right now. Your vision scope is the parameters set by the visionary about how far you want to go. Know your scope- including the people you want to meet or reach, places you want to go, and goals you want to see accomplished.

At some point in the day, your thoughts should reveal your focus on your vision.

All Power, All Sacrifice

Matthew 28:18 (KJV) says, *"All power has been given to me in heaven and earth."* Jesus was given "All Power" because He became all sacrifice. What you become is directly connected to what you will or will not give up. You will find out that, to become all, you must become all sacrifice. In other words, you should give up something to get something. In the great kenosis passage in Philippians 2:7, the scripture says that Christ "emptied Himself."

In theology, the term kenosis comes from the Greek word for the doctrine of Christ's emptying of self at the incarnation. It does not mean that He emptied Himself of deity. Rather it was a self-renunciation of His divinity so He could take on the form of a servant.

Jesus left His celestial splendor for this terrestrial to build a bridge for humankind to get to God. He took on the form of a servant so He could be relevant to our earthly experience. And because He did this, He was exalted for all time.

Jesus said, *"Take up your cross and follow me."* The cross is not supposed to make us self-centered, but it is the greatest object of servant leadership. Jesus was the ultimate example of humility in leadership. He has set a standard that has been distorted and redefined too many times. To truly be effective as servant leaders, we must free ourselves from the pride that so often grips the heart. Only then can our hearts be a chamber for His presence and power.

James 4:6 (KJV), says, *"But he giveth more grace. Wherefore he saith, God resisteth the proud, but giveth grace unto the humble."* What strikes you when you think of the word "pride?" Can there be a negative or a positive connotation associated with it? There are positive and negative types of pride. Some people take pride in their alma mater or in the fact that their son is going to college. Then there is the type of pride that is laced with superiority, arrogance, and dignity; this is the type God rejects.

God rejects the proud but gives grace or favor to the humble. Because of such toxic elements that make up the negative aspect of pride, God rejects it altogether. You can never have an advantage with pride in the heart. Humility always keeps the Grace of God active in your life.

Just Go

Going to the unknown requires faith and faith alone. Faith is the tool that brings people into their Promised Land, not money, notoriety or even fame. What God has for you is already prepared. You just have to obey Him and start moving. You will know that God is moving you when he tells you to leave what you know as your place of establishment. You have already adjusted to a routine. You wake up a certain time and eat your breakfast at a specific time. You see, that reality has trained you to exist in a world that someone has created.

Have you ever considered what your life would be like if you did as God commanded you to do? How much success could you achieve? How many lives could you touch with your gift?

Abraham left his comfort zone, the place of his father's dream, so he could find his space. Sometimes you have to leave what was stable for someone else and find your stability, it means taking a risk even when you did not see the end results. God tells Abram to, "Go! No address and no zip code! Just move at my word, and as you go, I will show you."

For Abram to become God's idea, he had to leave another man's reality. Could it be that another person's reality is stifling your productivity? Your personal growth has been stunted, you are not producing, and if you stay where you are expected to stay, your Sarai will not produce. (See Genesis 11:31–21, 12:1.) I believe that, when Abram obeyed God's word, not only did he begin his change process,

I believe that Sarai's womb opened. The key to leaving your barren place to a place of fruitfulness is obedience.

The advantage that obedience brings is that, when you obey God, you do not have to worry about the next step. God told Abram, "I am going to bless you and make your name great. You are going to be a blessing."

The Advantage of Now, Not Next!

Your next is waiting for a decision in your now.
—Ramon O. Gordon

What's next, or what now? You will need courage and determination to take advantage of the season that God currently has you in. That only means that you must rise to a level of accountability for the actions that must be taken moving forward. When you assume responsibility for your life, a plan of action must be put in place as you march on the pathway of life toward success. Real success does not have a prerequisite, a pedigree, or even a formula. Simply the combination of determination and hard work makes success. To have a "next" mentality, you must have a "prepare now" urgency.

At the 1963 march on Washington, Dr. King coined the message, "The Fierce Urgency of Now," which echoed the need for the immediacy of the government's response to inhumane acts against people of color. Although this speech was given fifty-five years ago, the essence of its message is interwoven with the spiritual destinies of men. Will you sit idly by this year and forsake the highway of purpose for the trail of contentment, or will you use the power of resilience and produce the greatness you were meant to produce?

The Bible says the righteous are as bold as a lion. (See Proverbs 28:1.) It's time to be bold about your purpose! To be bold implies a

The Advantage of Now

willingness to get things done despite the risks. And anywhere you discover purpose; you will find risk lurking nearby. Somehow the two are servants to each other, and risk is that offender who breaks the rules and goes against the status quo. Quite often, our purpose can remain in a passive state in our minds cradled in indecision and fear. But purpose-minded people are inherently risk takers. They are trendsetters, trailblazers, and deal breakers. These individuals are bold, even in the midst of failure. They boldly approach the challenge, and they boldly fail, if they have to.

If you listen carefully to your heart, you will find the inner rhythm of your destiny in sync with your frustrations and your anxieties. You see, sometimes our frustrations can be produced not by being stagnant but by our desire to progress. Frustration is defined as the feeling of being upset or annoyed, especially because of the inability to change or achieve something. Some things frustrate you not because of your failure to achieve, but because there are some phases that our will to continue must be tested. Staying frustrated cannot produce the change you desire. Only acknowledging the source of our frustration will do so. Perhaps God is wooing you out of inaction into the consciousness of that powerful person that you know you are. Listen to that rhythm and listen closely. There you will find God's plan for your next move.

I was raised in tropical places like Jamaica and Miami; hurricanes are common in those places. When the meteorologist would predict a hurricane, preparation would follow not long after. Whether it was a category one or five storm, it didn't matter because the storm sequence could change in a matter of moments. The travesty would be to assume that the storm would be small and ineffective, only to wish you had prepared beforehand. The path to destiny requires that we cooperate with God through preparation. Your willingness to go through the discipline of preparation is a sign of maturity acknowledging that change is taking place within your spirit.

On August 24, 1992, Hurricane Andrew, a category five storm, struck South Florida. At the time of its occurrence, it was the most destructive storm the United States had seen. Hurricane Andrew

Ramon O. Gordon

began as a tropical wave off the coast of Africa on August 14, 1992, and ten days later, winds of 175 miles per hour ravaged Southern Florida. Houses were flattened like pancakes. Roads were hidden under debris. Here is a segment of a Miami-Dade County Grand Jury Report:

> "The lack of adequate preparation by our community and our state was apparent. Even more noticeable was the total lack of coordination that existed between the various disaster relief agencies after the hurricane had passed. No one was in charge. No one knew what to do. There was no plan. As a result, a large segment of our community that had been reduced to a "third world" existence remained that way."

Even though the storm was destined to arrive in South Florida on that fateful day, had there been adequate preparation and coordination, the aftereffect might not have been so horrific. Also, a recovery time might have been more realistic. Some storms come into our lives to test our readiness. Perhaps you have just come through a storm, and another storm may be resurfacing, but don't despair. Maybe the storm is just testing your readiness and evaluating your lessons learned from storms prior.

Your underestimation can ignore a wave, and you end up in a category five storm, simply because your underestimation fooled you out of preparation. Do not become a victim of underestimation. Prepare for that sermon as if your life depends on it. Build that business with one employee until it you can hire more. Build on those godly principles early so your character can withstand the trials that life will bring.

You can underestimate a wave and end up with a storm. Similarly, you can underestimate a carpenter's son and end up with a Messiah, or you can underestimate a boy born in Hawaii to a white mother and a black father who ended up becoming President of the United States.

Not only does underestimation reveal a lack of preparation, in fact, it also shows the level of value we have for whatever or whoever

The Advantage of Now

crosses our paths. (See Romans 2:11). Never underestimate the power of God to take what is small in the eyes of others and make it big. The famous Aesop's fable, Tortoise and the Hare, highlights the value of underestimation. The hare is very confident and boastful and decides to take a nap after advancing deep into the race, only to wake up and find that the tortoise, moving slowly and steadily, has already arrived at the finish line. People will underestimate the progress you are making because of the pace you are going, but a steady pace and fixed resolve always puts you at the finish line. Know your limitations and move at your pace- you may not get there when everyone else does, but you will finish.

Peter and John could have easily ignored the man at the gate beautiful. After all, he was just a beggar who was lame from his mother's womb. (See Acts 3.) Society had no regard for such a man. Had Peter and John underestimated him because of his position, they would have missed out on being used as spiritual tools to restore that man to wholeness. But because the value was placed on his person, Peter says, *"Silver and gold have I none; but such as I have give I thee: In the name of Jesus Christ of Nazareth rise up and walk."* See Acts 3:6 (KJV).

If you value the moment, although it may cause some pain, it will yield dividends in knowledge that are priceless. Consider those profits as investments toward your future.

Watch Your Priorities

All of us have been guilty of this one word, "procrastination," a lethal delay of action that can threaten our progression forward into productivity. Procrastination is a bad habit, and whether we believe it or not, we find a way to justify this behavior. A primary key in identifying this negative behavior is to set a list of our priorities and divide them into two sections. One section is major; the other is minor.

No matter how simple or arduous that priority may seem, it needs to be placed in the proper location of importance in your life. Failing to do so can result in further delay of accomplishing your goals. Once you have set aside an honest list of your priorities, you have to now engage in the execution of the specific tasks required to fulfill each priority.

For example, a secondary priority may be to do your household chores, but you cannot get it accomplished when you are planted in front of the television most of the day. And a top priority may be to get your child to an important doctor's appointment, but you end up leaving home late because you did not have your clothes or the baby's things prepared the night before. The lack of preparation will show up on the day of execution while you regret not preparing the day before. You will live in regret if preparation is not viewed as a necessary step to success.

Prepare the day before. There are no absolute guarantees in life. Life is full of surprises that can alter daily routines. But the element of surprise should not be an excuse for lack of preparation. To live with this mindset will defeat the purpose of your efforts. Defeat does not always mean lack of readiness. Consider the scores of professional athletes who prepared tirelessly for a sports event weeks or even months before, only to be met with defeat. It does not mean failure, it simply increases a sense of work ethic and readjustments. Proverbs 24:27 (KJV) says, *"Prepare thy work without, and make it fit for thyself in the field; and afterwards build thine house."*

Add someone in your life who is smarter and wiser, someone who can help to hold you accountable as you navigate through life's challenges. Just choosing anyone will not do. Select someone who has been where you are trying to go so you can be pushed in the right direction. Get around people who will challenge you to be, do, and even expect better. If you want to produce a better quality of character, you should surround yourself with people who have quality. You cannot expect to produce remarkable things if you have people of substandard quality in your circle. In many ways, who you are connected to determines your altitude in life.

The path to destiny requires that you end mediocre excuses and swap it out with an expectation of excellence. Let your destiny be the magnet that connects you to the greatness in other people. Not only does this confirm your purpose, but it also affirms the sense of significance you have been experiencing for a long time.

Prioritize your goals, so it reflects your purpose. Once you know what your goals are, it becomes clear to you and everyone around that you where you are heading in your life. You are not confused about your goals, that mindset wants to dominate your mental space, but it is not so. Be honest about where you are in life. Then make the necessary adjustments to strengthen your current foundation, or maybe the base you are on is no longer sturdy enough to handle your expanding purpose. Some places that God plants you in are temporary character builders so that you can get ready for your next assignment.

Tell me. Which plant uproots itself once it has been planted it? None! In the same sense, God is the only one who can uproot what He plants. If you are still rooted in a place, it means there is more for you to learn and experience. Once God is ready to do His thing in your life, He will do it. When God moves you, He does so with the roots included, which represent your experiences.

A few years ago, somebody brought my father an avocado plant from Jamaica. It was a young plant. When that plant came to us, it already had roots since it had already been planted. All my father had to do was replant it. We have had a love-hate relationship with that tree for years, but it has been good to us. Like that plant, when God is redirecting you, He always includes the roots. The roots are the experiences you encounter in your life's journey. Life will shift you into new seasons, and those seasons have new soil. When you are planted in the soil of your new season, you have the advantage of your experiences to make you a success. Keep your roots, because they become the substratum for a healthy future.

Stable Thinking Produces Conscious Moves

You must safeguard the way you think if you are going to stretch to the finish line. From time to time, we will encounter challenges that are designed to set us off course, but never become blinded by the trial that you cannot see the God of the test. The right perspective will safeguard the right mentality to go through your challenges. It also creates the proper attitude to achieve proper destiny-fulfilling goals. Storms are a part of life. Those challenges prepare you for your purpose. See your storms as an opportunity to gain wisdom and insight into your life's journey and not inconvenient interruptions that serve no value.

Now is the time to stabilize yourself for change, growth, and expansion. The finish line is before you, and you are going to need all your strength to complete the task you have set on your priority list. The scripture says, *"a double-minded man is unstable in all his ways."* (See James 1:8 (KJV). The mind must be stable if it is going to execute the will of the God. The lack of stability with no firmness or soundness of thought fosters confusion. Now is not the time to be irresolute, but with firm conviction, move in the power of your faith. Identify your gifts, pray, and then move forward with the power of God all around you.

Listen to Caleb

When your life is in transition, who and what you listen to matters. You just cannot listen to everybody. The book of Numbers recounted the narrative when the children of Israel were on the verge of the land of Canaan. It recounts the many failures of the children of Israel and God's judgment because of His wrath. It should be a story depicting their triumphal entry into Canaan; rather it is a tale of them marching to the borders of the Promised Land only having to wait for an entire generation of Israelites to die off.

Numbers chapter 13 puts the children of Israel at the southern borders of Canaan, and the spies who were sent by Moses brought back a negative report about what they saw in the land. The children of Israel listened, but they listened to the wrong information. Be careful what you listen to because it can affect what you already heard from God. You heard, *"No weapon formed against you shall prosper* (See Isaiah 54:17)," but you are listening to the threats that your enemies

The Advantage of Now

hurled toward you. You heard, "With his stripes, we are healed (See Isaiah 53:5)," but you are listening to the bad report from the doctor. What you listen to can always affect what you already heard from God. There were giants in the Promised Land. The opposition seemed hard, and the odds were insurmountable. Because of what they heard, they rebelled against Moss and Aaron. (See Numbers 14: 1-3)

Listen to Caleb! Caleb in the Old Testament was one of the spies that Moses sent from Kadesh in southern Palestine to spy on the land of Canaan. He did not allow the presence of giants to intimidate his faith but urged the Israelites to seize the moment. (See Numbers 13:33.) Caleb's faith was uncanny and coupled with a now mentality; he was poised to take that moment. Sadly, the men who accompanied Caleb deflated the possibility of going to possess the Promised Land because of what they saw with their eyes.

Look at the response from the other spies who went along with Caleb to search out the land of Canaan. Numbers 13:31–33 (KJV) reads,

> "But the men that went up with him said, we be not able to go up against the people; for they are stronger than we. And they brought up an evil report of the land which they had searched unto the children of Israel, saying, the land, through which we have gone to search it, is a land that eateth up the inhabitants thereof; and all the people that we saw in it are men of a great stature. And there we saw the giants, the sons of Anak, which come of the giants: and we were in our own sight as grasshoppers, and so we were in their sight."

Here are three things to consider:

1. They give their opinion rather than an observation.
2. A concerted effort was made to discourage the people.
3. They exaggerated and fabricated a myth about the giants in the land.

Ramon O. Gordon

It amazes me, every time I read this, how the spies saw themselves. *"We were in our own sight as grasshoppers, and so we were in their sight."* Grasshopper thinking is a thought pattern that is laced with fear and insecurities. This is the season to have a giant killer mentality, not a grasshopper mentality. This is how the spies saw themselves, and they unfairly imposed their assessment of themselves on the children of Israel. God made them giant killers, but fear reduced them to think little of themselves in their mind. No matter what other people said about you, you are on the level of your best thought.

Make sure you have a Caleb in your circle when the time comes to strategize for promise possession. Caleb is that optimist who is not afraid of the challenge, but he sees the challenge as an opportunity for victory. Caleb's instinct to conquer dominated the instinct of fear. Out of all the men who went out to spy on the land, only Caleb saw the opportunity. And because of his faith, Caleb ended up possessing the land, not just him, but also his descendants. When you move in faith and not fear, God will make sure that not only do you receive the blessing, He will make it so everything connected to you will get the blessing. (See Numbers 14:24.)

Your inner circle should be a mixture of individuals who bring a positive outlook to the task. Everyone should not be "yes men," but you need people who are not afraid to seize the moment. Administer a Caleb test every now and then. Suggest a goal that seems far-reaching and ridiculous. This sort of test will reveal the heart of the people in your circle, especially if the goal is time-sensitive.

Your internal compass has you in proximity to your next blessing, only to be deflated by the fear and cynicism from people on your team. The Caleb test doesn't necessarily mean that you dismiss those who aren't in agreement. It can simply be an opportunity for you to release your spirit to those who you lead.

The spies allowed what they saw (sight) to affect what they believed (faith). At some point in our lives, our faith in what God said must have power over what we see. Sink your teeth into that next opportunity, and with unapologetic boldness, you will win the challenge.

Key Points:

- The thing that is restricting your move into success is not your potential. It is your mentality. When fear invades your mental space, you become stuck at the borders of greatness of greatness wandering around aimlessly.
- The border is never the destination. It is the beginning of the world of unseen fulfillment for you.
- Many people are stuck at the borders of greatness, considering their potential selves only dreaming about what could be, but never seizing the opportunity to go over and possess the promise of God.
- You cannot discover your greatest potential if you are only able to view the possibilities from the outskirts of inaction.
- You must engage if you are going to enlighten, empower, and enrich.
- Between promise and possession are choices. Make wise choices.

Bad Investments Don't Decide Value

Just recently in December 2016, Forbes put Warren Buffet as the second-richest man in America, as he was worth an estimated $73.9 billion. Warren Buffett is known as the Oracle of Omaha, and to many, he's a hero in the world of business. However, Mr. Buffett, amid his great success, has made bad investments. The one notable investment blunder is what he calls his "$200 billion mistake," his purchase of Berkshire Hathaway, an investment company that engages in diverse business activities including property and casualty, insurance and reinsurance, utilities and energy, and a host of other services. Buffett personally owned stock in the company and believed that assets in the company would make good investments. After some fallout after a deal went bad, feelings got in the way, and rash decisions were made. Although the company is thriving today, it still serves as an example of how unchecked emotions can provoke poor investment decisions.

That is in the world of business, but many of us have made poor investments in our personal lives. The key is not to let the investment define your value. What defines you is your ability to use poor choices as a catalyst for better conscious decision-making. Although it was a poor investment for Mr. Buffett, it did not decrease his value or delay his pace to becoming one of the most financially successful men on the planet. You cannot escape the effects of past decisions, but you can aim to be transformed by those decisions with a positive view forward. You may find that your past will seek to interfere with your progress but never respond to the past. Keep in your mind the eternal constant declaration that, "you are an overcomer."

Having proper self-worth is the right place to start, and how we chose to define our self-worth can directly affect how we view ourselves and, ultimately, God. The lessons we learn from failed places only help to shape our perspectives going into the next idea.

Avoid Conformity

> *"Here's to the crazy ones. The misfits. The rebels. The troublemakers. The round pegs in the square holes. The ones who see things differently. They're not fond of rules. And they have no respect for the status quo. You can quote them, disagree with them, glorify or vilify them. About the only thing you can't do is ignore them. Because they change things. They push the human race forward. And while some may see them as crazy ones, we see genius. Because the people who are crazy enough to think they can change the world, are the ones who do."*
> —Apple Computers: Think Different Ad Campaign, 1997

A conformist conforms to accepted behavior or established practices. To conform to something is to be identical in form or type or to agree or be in harmony with. Avoid conforming to standards that do not endorse the direction you are trying to go, which sometimes means avoiding people whose standards reflect poor integrity. Do you know what is acceptable to you? Or have you allowed your standards to fall victim to compromise? The path to destiny is too authentic for compromise, or too original for counterfeits. You cannot continue to conform to what you know is unacceptable to you, or you will end up a bitter conformist who never lived a life of transformation.

Rollo May, the American existential psychologist, said, *"The opposite of courage in our society is not cowardice, it is conformity."* It is becoming increasingly difficult to find originality in our society today. The truth is that many people are famous for their pulchritude or a few off-script blunders on television. While entertainment is a good form of escapism from the heavy demand of everyday life, what we are entertained by can be detrimental to our outlook on life. We can become so busy watching people live that we subconsciously pattern our lives according to what we see.

So stop watching and start being. The more time you spend conforming to something else, the less time you have to become what you know you can become. (See Acts 17:28). Conforming to anything other than God's plan is entirely antithetical to his will. God's intent and only intent has only been for you to become His idea.

My friends, I believe that God wants you to live a life of transformation. The radical act of transformation often brings the sharp pangs of scrutiny. Paul was a Jew who persecuted the early church but would end up on the other side of history as one of the greatest voices in the early church. On numerous occasions, the Apostle had to defend his calling, *"For you have heard of my previous way of life in Judaism, how intensely I persecuted the church of God and tried to destroy it"* (Galatians 1:13 NIV). After Paul's encounter with Jesus on the road to Damascus, his life would take a turn, and the history of the church would change for all time. His life was totally and unequivocally transformed.

The Greek word for "transform" is meta morphoo, which means change after being with or changing form in keeping with inner reality. The Apostle Paul was not one of the disciples who walked with Jesus. He was not there for the feeding of the five thousand or the transfiguration of Jesus Christ. He did not have that privilege; however, he had a revelation of the Lord that would make him a leading proponent of the Christian church in the New Testament. Revelation knowledge always sets you apart; it is the highest level of divine truth.

Advantage Requires Wisdom

"The ants are a people not strong, yet they provide their food in the summer" (Proverbs 30:25 ESV). There is a myriad of lessons in the experience on the ant. This scripture sheds light on a little thing to bring illumination to a great principle. Ants might not have the strength of the average human being, yet they can lift something twenty times their own size. The ant functions at its level with accuracy and precision. What may seem like a limitation is actually the strength that the ant uses to its benefit.

Preparation is the rule of provision. The ant prepares for winter during the summer months. They are a calculated set of creatures that live and move with synergy. It avoids the trap of procrastination. It does not waste its energy being idle, but it is disciplined in its routine until the goal is achieved.

Your season does not have to be here for you to be in a state of preparation. It should be that, when the season comes, you are in a place to execute at a greater level because your focus is not on what you did not do. Starting early is not overrated. Often the failure of waiting too late many times cheats us of great opportunities. The ant teaches us that advantage is good, but wisdom fuels this perspective. My mother would tell me a proverb when I was a young boy. She said, *"A stitch in time saves nine."* The proverb means that a prompt effort will prevent more work later.

Ants exemplify team leadership. Have you ever seen an ant with a breadcrumb in its mouth? It carries something fifty times its size, and when that crumb is too burdensome, it becomes a shared responsibility in the colony. Nothing can disrupt their synergy once momentum is built. If there is a disruption, they will build around it, no matter how great or small. What an attitude! What we learn from the ant is so valuable. No one is an island. The inner connectivity of key relationships helps to forward the efforts of a team.

On the path to living the purpose-filled life, time is essential, but our decisions become the foundation that positions us with the right advantage. Some decisions we make have no impact on our path to destiny but there are those crucial decisions can either make us or break us apart. In no way should we have a nonchalant attitude toward what we decide, but each choice must be thought and seasoned with prayer. I highly doubt, if you choose to wear red instead of blue today, it would negatively impact your purpose. Some of our concerns are irrelevant to our goals and desires.

We also tend to overly spiritualize things, not realizing that God is seen in the practical. Consequently, we stress ourselves over simple things and end up stuck, frustrated, and mentally debilitated. This is not God's will. Instead, His will is that we approach life with a clear head, knowing a submitted will to Him will only create the maximized life. When you know it is your time, it becomes your responsibility to make the right choice. Those choices will, in turn, give you the advantage.

You must become an active partner with God on the earth concerning your destiny. In your quest for dream fulfillment, understand the time you have been given by your creator is your window of opportunity. Remember, time never gives its opinion. It simply carries us on this current called life. Therefore, you must challenge yourself to meet your goals. What you choose to do with the time you have remaining will decide the life you will live. Choose the destiny path, because you are on the brink of change.

About the Author

Raised in a Christian home by loving parents, Ramon O. Gordon developed a love for Jesus Christ at an early age. God has blessed his ministry to expand and reach throughout the United States as well as around the world where God has used him in a special way in the gifts of the Spirit to bring deliverance to His people. The times demand a response to such antagonism towards this generation of believers, because of this awareness he believes that he is called to be a voice in this generation. He is married to the beautiful Abigail Gordon and they have three children, Emma, Beverly, and Olivia.